Major Contributors to Social Science Series

ALFRED MC CLUNG LEE, General Editor

Vilfredo Pareto

JOSEPH LOPREATO

University of Connecticut

THOMAS Y. CROWELL COMPANY

New York, Established 1834

ACKNOWLEDGMENTS

To Mr. Philip Allen, president of the Pareto Fund, for permission to re-
print the excerpts from Pareto's *Treatise*.

To the University of Chicago Press, for permission to use in the Introduction, with appropriate revisions, parts of Joseph Lopreato's "A Functionalist Reappraisal of Pareto's Sociology," *The American Journal of Sociology*,
LXIX (May, 1964), 639–46.

Editor's Foreword

Undergraduates often find a great challenge in reading a seminal thinker's major contributions to social science in their original form. But students are usually offered either volume-length works containing stimulating passages embedded in outworn discussions, or brief excerpts included with those of other authors in general collections of readings. The longer works tend to be repetitious and wordy, and some now appear misguided. At the same time, excerpts in general collections do not give enough of a contributor's work to make him come alive.

In planning the present series, John T. Hawes, Director of the College Department of the Thomas Y. Crowell Company, and I sought manuscripts free from either of the above weaknesses. The editors were asked to dig out the main lines of a contributor's method and thought from the verbiage and the dated materials obscuring them, and to make available, in one slim volume, a critical essay together with the most significant and interesting passages in a contributor's writings. The volumes in the series, considered as a whole, thus give the student an understanding of the diverse ways of thought that have gone into the making of the social science discipline as we now know it.

The series has been edited and written so that each little book can be read for its own merits and without need of additional props. Each contains the seminal ideas of an author which still remain alive today but does not gloss over his weaknesses. Each book provides a critical vignette of the social scientist as he is now seen. Each book, too, should be interesting to college sophomores and especially to undergraduate majors in the various social sciences.

What all volumes in the series have in common is an educative conception. They are all efforts to interest undergraduates in some of the great "originals" of social science and thus to stimulate further exploration of important ideas and methods. The editor-critic who has done each volume has been free to follow his own professional judgment in analyzing his major contributor and in selecting significant excerpts from his works. Each volume thus has an individuality deriving from its editor-critic as well as from its subject.

The books in this series are intended to enrich introductory courses in the various social sciences. For more advanced courses, they will permit the student to become acquainted with the meatiest contributions of many selected social scientists rather than the few whose works he might read more extensively. Advanced students will find these books invaluable for the purposes of review.

ALFRED MC CLUNG LEE

Preface

This book differs from other works on Pareto in one very important respect: the better part of it is neither a digest nor a critique. The preparation of it has been inspired by the recognition that while Pareto is undeniably a monumental figure in the development of sociological theory, his chief sociological work, the *Treatise*, is much too long to suit present needs and time availabilities. What we have been in want of for a long time is a short Pareto. The present volume is designed to meet this need. It consists of a critical essay, in which I discuss some of Pareto's fundamental ideas, and of a collection of representative excerpts in Pareto's own words.

Pareto's famous *Treatise* is the only one of his works represented in this volume. My aim, however, has been to pick the gist of his entire sociological argument. Beyond this, the intention has been to reveal Pareto's richness of thought and rigor of exposition so as to demonstrate the profound learning experience that lies in store for him who ventures into a full reading of the *Treatise*. I also hope that my endeavor will help, in some measure, to dismiss once and for all some of the absurd myths that in recent decades have tended to push Pareto's brilliant sociology into increasingly remote corners of sociological history. Two aspects of his sociology deserve particular attention by the sociologist and by his cousins in other social sciences: his extremely thorough contribution to what has since come to be known as "sociological functionalism," and his happy utilization of a general sociological model that synthesizes both consensus and coercion theories. Accordingly, these two topics have been the object of special attention in the introduction.

While the book will be found very useful for many introductory and advanced courses in such varied disciplines as sociology, political science, economics, history, philosophy, logic, and speech, it will have special applications to courses in sociological and political theory, political sociology, social stratification, social control, the sociology of organization and social change. In each of these areas the student will appreciate the logical rigor of Pareto's arguments, his uncommon erudition, his penetrating comprehension of the social phenomenon, and the elegance and mastery with which he upholds the sociological perspective in his critique of some of the foremost luminaries of Western philosophy.

The excerpts have been organized in five chapters, and with few exceptions they follow the original sequence. Chapter 1, which follows the Introduction, consists of a discussion of non-logical conduct and some methodological considerations. Chapter 2 contains the classification of the residues and a discussion of as many of these as space permitted. Likewise, Chapter 3 comprises the classification of derivations and illustrations of a few of them. Chapter 4 then gathers various excerpts about residues and derivations discussed together. Finally, Chapter 5 brings together numerous passages about the social system and its various aspects and properties, such as equilibrium, interdependence, utility, the use of force, speculators and *rentiers*, and social heterogeneity and circulation.

The readings are reproduced as they appear in Pareto, except for (1) some headings which I have provided; (2) figures, which have been renumbered; (3) Pareto's textual references to his own paragraph numbers, which in most cases have been freely deleted; (4) finally, textual transitions which have been provided in brackets, where abridgments have required them.

The following have given encouragement in the preparation of the book, or have helpfully commented on the Introduction: Ernest Becker, Alfred McClung Lee, Kurt H. Wolff, and Carolyn H. Lopreato, my wife, who also cheerfully contributed her typing skill to the undertaking. Their help and suggestions, though not always heeded, are sincerely appreciated.

J. L.

Storrs, Connecticut
February, 1965

Contents

Vilfredo Pareto

Introduction: A Reappraisal
of Pareto's Sociology

A quarter century ago Pareto was one of the most discussed theorists in social science. Today, although his ideas have not completely disappeared from the sociological forum—they are readily noticeable in the writings of Parsons, Merton, Homans, and Levy among other major scholars—few in sociology read Pareto. To be sure, the fact (though not necessarily the substance) of his contributions is generally recognized in references to society as a social system as well as in discussions of elite circulation. But even here there are those who would prove Pareto's analyses to be superfluous. Thus, in discussing studies of "power-wielding elites" Lipset and Bendix feel justified to suggest en passant that "this approach is usually associated with Pareto's theory of the elite, but it was given a striking formulation almost two centuries earlier by Bernard Mandeville." [1] Aside from my failure to

[1] Seymour M. Lipset and Reinhard Bendix, *Social Mobility in Industrial Society* (Berkeley: University of California Press, 1959), p. 114. Attempts to discredit Pareto have been numerous, and sometimes bizarre or even rancorous. Most recently, after providing the reader with an amusing analysis of Pareto's personality and yet while searching for scientific prejudices in his sociology, Werner Stark has complained that Pareto was a "nuisance" as a "Newton of the Moral World." Pareto's "mechanistic," "artificially constructed model" of the social system seems to Stark so unrealistic that it not only has contributed nothing to sociology but "has also inhibited the advancement of our knowledge of economic reality." This is so despite the fact that "in economics his fame is as secure as it is insecure in sociology." See Werner Stark, "In Search of the True Pareto," *The British Journal of Sociology*, XIV (June 1963), 103–112. Of course, Stark adduces no substantial evidence in support of his interesting assertions, and he offers no help to the reader who might take it upon himself to learn what nonartificial models might be.

1

see Mandeville's "striking formulation" in the passage quoted by the authors (pages 114–15), I find it difficult to share their view of the history of ideas, for if pushed to the extreme, it might well result in a shocking pauperization of present endeavors. Nevertheless, their assessment of Pareto serves to demonstrate that Pareto's most critical contributions lie ignored in different areas of sociology. In my judgment, the recognized aspects of his thought are mere manifestations of more fundamental, more original concerns in his sociology.

It is no secret that Pareto's famous analysis of society in terms of an equilibrium theory owes much to previous scientific formulations, notably to that by the chemist Willard Gibbs. Similarly, his treatment of elite circulation has several important precedents, among which are Mosca's and Kolabinska's. Therefore, Pareto's work in these areas, however considerable, is by no means remarkable. But there are at least two other critical and highly developed aspects of his sociology that wait to be fully discovered and utilized, and they correspond to the two major concerns of sociological inquiry in its continuing attempt to achieve full scientific maturity, namely: (1) the development of a theoretical system to explicate the long-standing conception of society as "a functional instrument" of adaptation by man to his habitat; and (2) the construction of a theoretical system that would adequately answer the fundamental question, "Why do societies cohere and endure?" It is my purpose to demonstrate in this essay and in the readings that follow that in both of these areas Pareto, with consummate skill and deliberation, took gigantic strides forward that are either unknown or minimized. I also propose that Pareto's sociology is worth a detailed and patient reading in order to avoid the digestion of muddled notions which have followed tortuous and corroding itineraries.

Pareto's Functionalism

In discussions of sociological functionalism we sometimes encounter interpretations of Pareto's work which are frankly puzzling, if not altogether ridiculous. Barring one or two exceptions, the general consensus seems to be that in Pareto's sociology there is at most only an embryo of functionalism. It is hoped that the present essay and the excerpts from Pareto that follow will help the informed reader to decide for himself whether Pareto's contributions to "functional analysis" are embryonic or fully developed. My intention here is not merely to demonstrate that Pareto was in some way a forerunner of sociological functionalism. (Such an attempt in itself might amount to an interesting exercise in the history of ideas, but to little more. I am fully aware that in order to grow, a science must rest its feet on the scaffold of the "systematics of theory" rather than on the colorful mosaics of the "history of theory.") My aim is to show that Pareto's functionalism is highly developed, systematic, and in many respects free of the snares that bedevil most current functionalist conceptions.

PARETO'S FUNCTIONALISM IN
THE LITERATURE

Let us first look at a few interpretations of Pareto on this score. Buckley finds "implicit functionalism in Pareto's thought" and proposes that "we may recognize a further external stimulus to functionalism, though less influential in this respect, in the work of the Italian Vilfredo Pareto." [2] Buckley then quickly proceeds to state that Pareto "did make some use of what we have come to call the functional method," and he quotes a passage from Henderson[3] that points out a close parallel between Pareto's notion of the utility of religion and the concept of "survival value" in biology. Also Martindale discerns a trace of functionalism in Pareto, and in addition to merrily labeling him a "positivistic" and "voluntaristic" "organicist," one who "approves" the use of "the most brutal force to crush innovation" and who theorizes that disorder is due to "a little group of agitators," [4] he informs us that Pareto was "a transitional figure between organicism and sociological functionalism," [5] and that since Pareto, functionalism has "evolved rapidly" in the works of Homans, Merton, Parsons, and the Parsonians, including Shils and Bales.[6]

But Parsons, who in addition to being an illustrious functionalist

[2] Walter Buckley, "Structural-Functional Analysis in Modern Sociology," *Modern Sociological Theory*, ed. H. Becker and A. Boskoff (New York: The Dryden Press, 1957), p. 238.
[3] Lawrence J. Henderson, *Pareto's General Sociology* (Cambridge: Harvard University Press, 1935).
[4] Don Martindale, *The Nature and Types of Sociological Theory* (Boston: Houghton Mifflin Company, 1960), p. 531.
[5] Ibid., p. 466.   [6] Ibid., p. 500.

is also one of Pareto's major American interpreters, sees no functional approach at all in Pareto's sociology. Thus his objective in The Social System is to "carry out Pareto's intention" to delineate the social system, following the "structural-functional" approach, "which is quite different from that of Pareto." [7] And Merton, who is certainly one of the foremost modern functionalists, makes no reference at all to Pareto in his famous essay on "manifest and latent functions," [8] though he does find room for Pareto somewhere else in his famous volume: in connection with his discussion of "functions of norms of pure science," Merton chastises Pareto in a small part of a footnote for his comment that "the quest for experimental uniformities is an end in itself." [9] Aside from the question of the propriety of Pareto's statement, the following pages attempt to show that there might be more appropriate places for Pareto in Merton's volume.

A welcome respite from this sort of treatment of Pareto is offered by Kingsley Davis, who, in discussing the distinction between manifest and latent functions, declares that "it was developed with extreme thoroughness in Pareto's discussion, in 1916, of individual utility and utility to, of, and for the community." [10]

In what sense of the word can we say that Pareto's approach is "functional"? This is a critical question, for as it has often been pointed out, there are several schools of thought laying claim to the title "functionalist." Although it is not possible at this time to present a comparison between Pareto and leading exponents of all these various schools, I can say that in my opinion Pareto's functionalism is most similar to the widely known form of functionalism best represented by Robert K. Merton.[11] For this reason, an occasional comparative reference will be made to the well-known functionalism of this scholar in order to facilitate understanding of the argument on

[7] Talcott Parsons, The Social System (Glencoe, Ill.: The Free Press, 1951), p. vii.
[8] Robert K. Merton, Social Theory and Social Structure (Glencoe, Ill.: The Free Press, 1957), ch. I. Merton states early in his essay (p. 19) his intention to "interweave our account with a systematic review of some of the chief conceptions of functional theory." In the light of evidence soon to be presented, it may later seem odd to the reader that Merton would not find even a "chief conception of functional theory" in Pareto's sociology.
[9] Ibid., p. 543, n. 22.
[10] Kingsley Davis, "The Myth of Functional Analysis as a Special Method in Sociology and Anthropology," American Sociological Review, XXIV (December 1959), 765.
[11] Op. cit.

Pareto. So far as I have been able to discover, the only basic functionalist differences between these two sociologists are three:

1. Merton has shown a preference for the analysis of concrete social structures such as ceremonials, political machines, bureaucracy, patterns of values, and science. But Pareto was mainly concerned with formulating a general functional theory of social structure. Again, Merton has preferred to give a perfecting glance to a few existing "functional conceptions," "codify" them, and demonstrate their increased usefulness in the explanation of various concrete social structures. Pareto, instead, emphasized the formal properties of theory construction, and consequently his most striking result was what the logician Northrop has justly called an "abstract theory" of social structure.[12]

2. While the basic starting point of Pareto's functional analysis is the delineation of the system, Merton appears to take the system as given by the generally accepted hypothesis of interdependence. His basic preference is in establishing the open-system proposition that any item, provided it be social (that is, repetitive and standardized), is subject to an analysis of its consequences for the larger structures in which it is implicated.

3. Merton has taken inspiration from the theory of the physiologist Walter B. Cannon, with all the problems that this involves for the specification of what Nagel has called "the vital functions" as "defining attributes" of social structures.[13] Pareto, instead, made use of the more restricted theory of equilibrium, which, as Northrop rightly observes,[14] Pareto borrowed from Willard Gibbs, having familiarized himself with the theory in his previous work on equilibrium in heterogeneous physical systems. This difference, as we shall see, had important consequences for the functional analyses of Merton and Pareto.

THE SOCIAL SYSTEM

Pareto's functionalism is an integral part of his view of society as a system tending toward an equilibrium. The central feature of his

---

[12] F. S. Northrop, The Logic of the Sciences and the Humanities (New York: The Macmillan Company, 1947), p. 272.
[13] Ernest Nagel, The Structure of Science (New York: Harcourt, Brace & World, 1961), p. 527.
[14] Op. cit., p. 266.

approach is the analysis of mutually dependent variations of the variables with which he focuses on the social system, together with the
analysis of the functions that these variables or "elements," singly
and in combination, discharge for the social system and for various
units implicated in it. Let us begin with Pareto's definition of the
system, which with characteristic scientific vigor he views in terms
of virtual movements and at a specific state of equilibrium:

If we intend to reason at all strictly, our first obligation is to fix upon
the state in which we are choosing to consider the social system, which is
constantly changing in form. The real state, be it static or dynamic, of
the system is determined by its conditions. Let us imagine that some
modification in its form is induced artificially. At once a reaction will
take place, tending to restore the changing form to its original state as
modified by normal change. If that were not the case, the form, with its
normal changes, would not be determined but would be a mere matter
of chance. [§2067] [15]

We can take advantage of that peculiarity in the social system to
define the state that we choose to consider and which for the moment
we will indicate by the letter X. We can then say that the state X is
such a state that if it is artificially subjected to some modification different from the modification it undergoes normally, a reaction at once takes
place tending to restore it to its real, its normal, state. That gives us an
exact definition of the state X. [§2068]

The question now arises of the real forces that determine a state of
equilibrium in the social system, namely, the "elements" that act
upon the system and in turn are reacted upon by it. Pareto distinguishes among three broad groups of them as follows: (1) soil,
climate, flora, fauna, and geological, mineralogical, and other conditions; (2) elements external to the system both in space, such as the
actions of other systems, and in time, such as the consequences of a
previous state of the system; (3) elements internal to the system,
such as sentiments, interests, attitudes, the state of knowledge, and
logical and pseudo-logical explanations. The task of taking into account all such elements is, at least for the present, impossible. Limitations are necessary, but much can be done within these limitations

[15] For the sake of convenience, and whenever possible, the quotations from Pareto
in this introduction are identified by a section number in brackets (or parenthe-
ses) following the quotation. These section numbers appear in Pareto's *Trattato
di Sociologia generale*, from which all the quotations are drawn. For brevity's
sake, we will refer to this work as the *Treatise* (see page 35).

(§2063). Accordingly, Pareto groups the multitude of elements into four principal categories:

1. Interests. These are largely the logical, goal-oriented elements of conduct that provide the basic data for the science of economics. They are not discussed in any detail in the Treatise.

2. Social heterogeneity and circulation. Today we might refer to this category as "class dynamics." Broadly speaking, it is concerned with social stratification and mobility, but Pareto deals with it in terms simplified enough to permit him to specify the basic mechanisms of equilibrium in the political structure.

3. Derivations. Pareto lists seventeen derivations, which he groups in four classes. They are the verbal utterances, assertions, appeals to authority, and rationalizations that represent man's hunger for logical explanations of his actions. However, given the overbearing force of "sentiments" (the non-logical, unpremeditated, self-acting, moral forces of human behavior), the explanations turn out in fact to be mostly pseudo-logical.

4. Residues. Of these Pareto enumerates a total of fifty-one basic ones, which he organizes into six classes. They are the manifestations of the fundamental action predispositions of men, that is, the sentiments or underlying forces of human conduct.

A word of caution is in order at this point. Pareto used a variety of terms as synonyms for sentiment and residue, not least of which is the word "instinct." As a result he has sometimes confused his readers and has often been misunderstood and criticized on this score. As a recent case in point, Schermerhorn and Boskoff see fit to hurl many curious hammers at Pareto: "Despite his apparent advocacy of scientific method, according to the consensus of critical accounts, Pareto often abused it in practice, exhibited unadorned political bias and an underlying anti-intellectualism, employed an 'instinct psychology' that was thoroughly discredited in the thirties, and, finally, contributed to sociology little that was not already available in the works of Freud, Marx, Mosca, and others." [16] Whatever Pareto may have called these primitives of his theory, a careful read-

---

[16] Richard A. Schermerhorn and Alvin Boskoff, "Recent Analyses of Sociological Theory," *Modern Sociological Theory*, ed. Becker and Boskoff, pp. 72–73 (italics added). Addressing myself to the sole question of "instinct psychology," it must be pointed out that the fact that Pareto used the term "instinct" is not *prima facie* evidence that he employed an "instinct psychology." Sometimes we unfortunately respond to the sound of a word rather than to its cognitive content.

ing of his Treatise would reveal that he posited no instinct psychology. His argument on the score is a lucid instance of rigorous scientific reasoning. Here is the irreducible core of his discussion:

So we shall say, simply, that residues are among the elements which determine the social equilibrium, a statement that must be translated and understood as meaning that "the sentiments manifested by residues are among the elements which stand toward the social equilibrium in a relationship of reciprocal determination." But that statement too is elliptical and has again to be translated. *Let us beware of ascribing any objective existence to our residues or even to sentiments.* What we observe in reality is a group of human beings in a mental condition indicated by what we call sentiments. Our proposition must, therefore, be translated in the following terms: "The mental states that are indicated by the sentiments expressed in residues are among the elements that stand in a relation of reciprocal determination with the social equilibrium." But if we would express ourselves in a language altogether exact, that is still not enough. What in the world are those "mental states" or, if one will, those "psychic conditions"? *They are abstractions.* And what underlies the abstractions? So we are obliged to say: "The actions of human beings are among the elements that stand in a relationship of reciprocal determination with the social equilibrium. Among such actions are certain manifestations that we designate by the term 'residues' and which are closely correlated with other acts so that once we know the residues we may, under certain circumstances, know the actions. Therefore we shall say that residues are among the elements that stand in a relation of reciprocal determination with the social equilibrium." [§1690—italics added]

Beyond this purely methodological level, another important interpretation of the concept of residue or sentiment (or instinct) is warranted. Some of the sentiments might properly be called "primary drives" today. This is the case, for instance, with the basic sex residue, which provides the sixth category in Pareto's classification of residues. Others may be more properly termed basic values or mores, deeply learned and entrenched. Such is the case with the "residues of sociality" and particularly with their sub-classes, "sentiments of hierarchy" and sentiments of "risking one's life." Here is one revealing statement on this question: "People risk or even sacrifice their lives out of deep feelings of sociality, or from the importance they attach to the esteem of others. . . . General Nogi, victor for the Japanese at Port Arthur, killed himself with his wife on the day of the Mi-

kado's funeral. In that case the sacrifice of life had no direct utility. It was a pure manifestation of sentiments of sociality, subordination, hierarchy, combined with certain group-persistences of the old-fashioned Samurai, and with a desire for the approbation of people sharing those sentiments" (§1148).

To be sure, Pareto's discussion of the sentiments is not always as cultural in nature as the above. There are times when he definitely prefers the word "instinct" to "sentiment" and even to "residue." At such times he would seem to put dogs, roosters, bulls, and the like on the same footing with man. Almost invariably, however, a very close look at his arguments reveals a thoroughly sociological interpretation. What happens in such cases is that Pareto is so impressed by the power of social forces that transcend human reason or motivation that he treats these forces as if they were biological instincts. One can hardly understand why he neglected a vast literature that would have more practically extricated him from this minor difficulty, notably the works of William G. Sumner and Walter Bagehot. What matters, however, is that at close scrutiny there is little doubt that very many "instincts" are treated by Pareto as deeply entrenched norms, or as Bagehot might say, as elements of a "cake of custom."

But beyond all these considerations, it must be kept in mind that for purposes of theory construction, the sentiments are merely assumed psychic states or forces and imply no psychological processes. It does not matter to the sociologist whether they are instinctual or learned, provided the social phenomena that suggest them are sociologically relevant. Pareto repeatedly warns that the terms "sentiment," "instinct," "need," "residue," and so on, are abstractions or convenient makeshifts in sociology, just as the term "force" has proved convenient in physics (§1690). His emphasis is never on the sentiments per se but on the social actions that suggest them to him in his scientific commitment to a taxonomy of the social phenomenon. His position on this score is analogous to Sumner's in his "socializing forces" and to W. I. Thomas' in his "four wishes." Pareto's classification, however, is more detailed.

Four, then, are the principal categories of elements that Pareto chooses to isolate for the analysis of social systems. They constitute his basic conceptual scheme. Throughout the Treatise they receive detailed examination and application, both singly and interdependently. *His analysis of "cycles of interdependence" among them—too long to discuss here—may well be the best existing example of a functional analysis (see especially §§2203–78).*

FUNCTION OR UTILITY

Underlying the four categories of elements as tools of sociological analysis we then find a very critical notion which has come to be known as the concept of "function." It leads to the very heart of Pareto's functionalism. Pareto formally introduces this concept in connection with his discussion of the organization of the social system. For him, function, "utility," or "effect," as he variously prefers to call it, is one of the major "properties of the social system":

A system of material atoms and molecules has certain thermic, electrical, and other properties. So a system made up of social molecules also has certain properties that it is important to consider. One among them has been perceived, be it in a rough and crude fashion, in every period of history—the one to which with little or no exactness the term "utility" or "prosperity," or some other such term, has been applied. We must now dig down into the facts to see whether something definite can be found underlying these vague expressions, and its character determined. [§2105]

After proposing that to get a more exact picture one must state just what norms he intends to follow in determining the entities he is trying to define, Pareto gives this technical definition of utility:

Once we have fixed upon the norms we elect to follow *in determining a certain state as the limit that an individual or a community is assumed to approach,* and once we have given numerical indices to the different states that more or less approximate the limit state, so that the state closest to it has an index larger than the index of the state farthest removed, we can say that those indices are indices of a state X. Then, as usual, for the purpose of avoiding the inconvenience of using mere letters of the alphabet as terms . . . and for no other reason, we shall apply the term "utility" to the entity X just described. [§2111—italics added]

In more concrete terms, the concept of utility has two basic, related meanings suggested by Pareto's recognition that society may be viewed both as an aggregate of human beings and as a social organization:

1. It may refer to a contribution that a given element or phenomenon makes to the maintenance or to the achievement of a given

goal or "satisfaction," real or assumed, of individuals or groups. Since this type of utility is viewed as flowing from a particular goal, it would be proper to speak of utilities as "manifest" or "latent functions," depending on whether or not the utility is in direct correspondence with the precedent goal.

2. Utility may refer to any significant, intentionless, and unobvious effect that a phenomenon has (or is capable of having under appropriate circumstances) on the maintenance of a stated, approximate condition in the social system in which the phenomenon occurs. On this second meaning of the term, Pierce has keenly observed in an enlightening essay on the functionalism of Durkheim that "the 'function' of a social phenomenon proves, in the last analysis, to be its causal contribution to the existing state of affairs." [17]

Each of these two types of utility must be considered from the viewpoint of the kind of contribution it makes. If the function is of "beneficial" value, Pareto prefers the general term "utility" for it. If it is "harmful," we have a "detriment." The following paragraph clearly shows Pareto's "modern look," while at the same time it evidences an obvious awareness of various considerations falling within the rubric of functional analysis:

To utilize the sentiments prevalent in a society for attaining a given purpose is in itself neither beneficial nor detrimental to society. The utility, or the detriment, depends upon the result achieved. If the result is beneficial, one gets a utility; if harmful, a detriment. Nor can it be said that when a governing class works for a result that will be advantageous to itself regardless of whether it will be beneficial or the reverse, to its subject class, the latter is necessarily harmed. Countless the cases where a governing class working for its own exclusive advantage has further promoted the welfare of a subject class. [§2249]

INTENTION AND FUNCTION, OR PURPOSE AND UTILITY

It may have been noted in the definition of the two types of function above that the difference between the two meanings may

[17] Albert Pierce, "Durkheim and Functionalism," Émile Durkheim, 1858–1917, ed. Kurt H. Wolff (Columbus: Ohio State University Press, 1960), p. 159. This definition also corresponds to the sixth of the various meanings of function discussed by Nagel, op. cit., p. 525.

*also be viewed in terms of the presence or absence of any purpose
involved in the phenomenon yielding the function. As is shown also
by several paradigms and numerous discussions in the* Treatise, *this
fact bears witness to Pareto's acute sensitivity to the distinction
between the purpose of a social action and its utility. Indeed in his
discussion of "theories" (that is, propositions or verbal statements)
the first distinction he makes early in the* Treatise *is that between
purpose and utility. In Pareto's own words:*

Given the proposition $A = B$, we must answer the following questions:
  1. *Objective aspect.*   Is the proposition in accord with experience, or is
it not?
  2. *Subjective aspect.*   Why do certain individuals assert that $A = B$?
And why do other individuals believe that $A = B$?
  3. *Aspect of utility.*   What advantage (or disadvantage) do the sentiments reflected by the proposition $A = B$ have for the person who states
it, and for the person who accepts it? What advantage (or disadvantage)
does the theory itself have for the person who puts it forward, and for
the person who accepts it? [§14]

The question of *objective aspect* is linked to the distinction between "logical" and "non-logical" action. It is therefore a question
regarding the relative efficiency of action, a conception that eventually suggests to Pareto notions of minima, maxima, and optima. Put
otherwise, it would help quantify the concept of utility and would
sharpen such concepts used by him as "harmful effect" and "beneficial effect" or such concepts as "eufunction" and "dysfunction"
still in use among more recent functionalists.

The *subjective aspect* refers to what some contemporary sociologists call "subjective dispositions." Pareto himself uses various terms,
for example, "ideal," "motive," and "purpose." He discusses a variety
of types of purposes, of which the following two are the major ones:
  1. There is, first, the "real purpose." This is a conscious force im-
pelling to clearly definable action that would result in clearly intended consequences.
  2. There is, next, what may be called an "instrumental purpose."
This differs from the real purpose mainly in that it is usually un-
reachable but is often necessary for achieving the real purpose. For
instance, in market transactions we often find that in order to receive what is considered a fair price, the seller asks more for his
product than he expects to get from the buyer. What Pareto is
doing here, of course, is raising the question, what is the purpose of

a purpose? This is in harmony with his concern with "discovering the substance underlying outward forms," a theme basic to all his search.

Indeed, his discussion of types of purpose is largely intended to sensitize the reader to the difficulty of taking human intentions into account in analyzing social action. All too frequently, overelaborated strata of apparent intentions conceal the real intentions—wherever these exist at all—and render difficult if not impossible the task of linking action with intention and, of course, intention with function. (See especially §§1867–96.) Pareto, therefore, would find it difficult to accept such a statement as this one in which Merton reveals a clearly "voluntaristic" strain: "At some point, functional analysis invariably assumes or explicitly operates with some conception of the motivation of individuals involved in a social system." [18]

But for still another reason Pareto would not agree with the foregoing proposition. As we can surmise from the definitions of utility presented above, Pareto clearly distinguishes between social action and social form. In the analysis of the former, the concern with motivation is often appropriate. In the analysis of the latter, it is usually superfluous or irrelevant, for the social form does not bear passively the operation of the elements that determine it. On the contrary it has a degree of autonomy of its own and, consequently, given the condition of interdependence, a degree of influence on them as well. Thus Pareto states: "When . . . a society is organized under a certain form that is determined by the other elements, it acts in its turn upon them, and they, in that sense, are to be considered as in a state of interdependence with it" (§2061). The social form, therefore, is capable of producing effects, or utilities, irrespective of human intentions.[19]

UNITS SUBSERVED BY FUNCTIONS, OR UTILITY FOR WHOM?

Having made the distinction between purpose and utility, Pareto now clarifies the heterogeneity of social units to be considered in appraising a given utility:

[18] Op. cit., p. 50.

[19] The point made here may also be judged with reference to Durkheim's analogous discussion of "social facts"; see Émile Durkheim, Les règles de la méthode sociologique (Paris: Félix Alcan, 1895).

The important thing, first of all, is to distinguish cases according as we
are thinking of the individual, the family, a community, a nation, the
human race. And not only are the utilities of those various entities to be
considered; a further distinction has to be drawn between their direct
utilities and the utilities that they derive indirectly through their mutual
relationships. So, disregarding other distinctions that it might be of advantage to make, and keeping to such as are absolutely indispensable,
we find ourselves obliged to deal with the following varieties:
a. *Utility to the Individual:*
   a-1. Direct
   a-2. Indirect, resulting from the fact that the individual is part of a
        community
   a-3. Utility to an individual, as related to the utilities to others
b. *Utility to a Given Community:*
   b-1. Direct utility to communities, considered apart from other com-
        munities
   b-2. Indirect utility, arising by reaction from other communities
   b-3. Utility to one community as related to the utilities to other com-
        munities. [§2115]

*Far from coinciding, these various utilities often stand in open oppo-
sition (§2115). In the functional analysis of a certain phenomenon
it is therefore necessary to specify the units for which that phenomenon has a given function. For society is "a heterogeneous affair and
that fact cannot be ignored" (§1882).*

*But Pareto goes beyond the specification of a range of units for
which a given phenomenon can have determinate functions. He
takes seriously the concept of interdependence, generally deemed
basic to functional analysis, and distinquishes between "direct"
utility and "indirect" utility. The former arises, with respect to an
individual, for instance, from the context of his own behavior. The
latter in turn arises from the fact that, as he is a member of a group,
the actions of others may have repercussions for his utilities.*

*With respect to the analysis of utilities to the community, Pareto
argues for a further refinement. He distinguishes between the utility
of a community and the utility for a community. The former refers
to the utility to the community as an organization, the latter to the
utility to the community as a collecivity of individuals. Take, for
example, the matter of population increase. As regards prestige and
military power, we allegedly approach a maximum utility of the
community as we increase population size to a point beyond which
"the nation would be impoverished and its stock decay." But a*

smaller population would mean a more commodious level of living, and to that extent we would have a high utility for the collectivity, that is, the various individual members of it (§§2131–35).

Finally, each of the types of utility mentioned in the above paradigm must also be considered with reference to time. What is very beneficial today may well be quite detrimental tomorrow, and vice versa. Thus, for instance, a policymaker must be forever on guard against the possibility that by eliminating a detrimental social form today he is not in effect destroying a greater future utility. As Pareto says: "The utility of today is frequently in conflict with the utility of days to come, and the conflict gives rise to phenomena that are well known under the names of providence and improvidence in individuals, families, and nations" (§2119).

MANIFEST AND LATENT FUNCTIONS, OR INTENDED AND INCIDENTAL EFFECTS

In brief, the chain of utilities of social actions and forms is for Pareto frequently long and very tortuous. Of all considerations arising essentially from this circumstance, one, which in recent years has come to be known as the "latent function," deserves particular attention. As Kingsley Davis has justly suggested, this concept is highly developed in Pareto's sociology. The idea emerges forcefully from three basic contexts:

1. As is well known, one of Pareto's major tasks was to demonstrate the preponderance of non-logical reasoning in society. This task is accomplished by way of his means-end scheme, a close examination of which reveals that the utilization of inappropriate means for reaching given goals is one possible source of the latent function. If the means employed for the achievement of certain goals are inappropriate, it follows that whatever effects these means may have are incidental or unintended.

2. Having demonstrated the preponderance of non-logical reasoning in society, Pareto was naturally led to ask why it was so widespread and accepted. The query in turn led him to distinguish between "the experimental truth" of an argument and its "social utility," adding that "correlation of the social utility of a theory with its experimental truth is in fact, one of those a priori principles which we reject" (§72). Indeed, in considering various types of theories

cross-classified in terms of (1) accord with experience, (2) accord with sentiments, (3) acceptance-rejection, and (4) utility, he explained the widespread acceptance of non-logical reasonings in terms of the utility that they have for various units in the society or for the social system as a whole (§14). And this is patently an expression of the latent function.

3. Finally, Pareto's focus on the latent function was a natural by-product of the hypothesis of interdependence in the social system.[20] For if the units constituting the system are interdependent, the repercussions of action or movement in one unit combine with movements in other units, modifying these to some extent and thus producing certain effects that in some degree differ from the effects that would have been observed if the individual units had been autonomous.[21]

The following statement, in which Pareto is discussing difficulties in lawmaking, concisely conveys his notion of latent function as an effect incidental to a specific purpose: "If . . . in working for a given objective, one is in a position to influence interests and sentiments, to modify them, the modification may have, in addition to the effects desired, other effects that are not in the least intended; so that one still has to consider both the intended and the incidental effects and see just what the social utility of their resultant will be" (§1864—italics added).[22]

[20] A passing reference to this point was made in the preceding treatment of the indirect utility.

[21] For a brilliant discussion of "cycles of interdependence," see Pareto, op. cit. (§§2203–78). For an excellent concrete example, see especially his discussion of "industrial protection" (§§2208–22). Interdependence and autonomy must, of course, be viewed in relative terms. The units or parts of a social system are not all equally interdependent with, or autonomous from, each other. This point is recognized and dealt with by Pareto in his discussion of cycles of interdependence, where he argues that the four elements of the system differentially influence each other and the equilibrium of the system, with the derivations having the least influence on the system or on any of the other three elements constituting it. The problems of relative autonomy, interdependence, and reciprocity have been recently recognized and formally discussed by Alvin W. Gouldner, "Reciprocity and Autonomy in Functional Theory," Symposium on Sociological Theory, ed. Llewellyn Gross (White Plains, N. Y.: Row, Peterson and Co., 1959), pp. 241–70.

[22] It might be noted in this connection that the term "incidental" preferred by Pareto is considerably more precise than the term "latent" used by Merton. Unlike "incidental," this latter term suggests that the effect is not active, perhaps even hidden or only potential, so that in terms of a semantic desideratum of

NET BALANCE OF FUNCTIONAL
CONSEQUENCES, OR NET UTILITY

It is the recognition of various types and degrees of utility that eventually suggests to Pareto a very important concept that seems identical to the concept of "net balance of functional consequences," so skilfully utilized by Merton to put to rest deeply entrenched but erroneous postulates of functional analysis.[23] Pareto's own concept, which hardly requires comment, comes out most clearly in the following statement, from which the reader may also surmise that when the concept is applied to the social system, it represents in fact a state of equilibrium in the system:

Net utility. Taking account of the three types of utility noted in the case of a single individual [see paradigm above], we get as a result the net utility that the individual enjoys. He may, on the one hand, suffer a direct damage and on the other hand, as a member of a community, secure an indirect advantage; and the latter may be so great as more than to offset the direct damage, so that in the end there is a certain gain for a remainder. So for a group. If we could get indices for these various utilities, and take their sum, we would have the total or net utility of the individual or group. [§2120] [24]

FUNCTIONAL PREREQUISITES AND
FUNCTIONAL ALTERNATIVES

Material is bountiful in the Treatise to demonstrate Pareto's timeliness and, in very many respects, eminent standing in the growing functionalist debate, which yet has curiously chosen to neglect him. But the point would seem to be established. I shall now conclude the discussion of Pareto's functionalism by dealing briefly with two other important aspects of functional analysis, namely, what Merton has referred to as "functional prerequisites" and "functional alternatives."

---

not doing violence to the meaning of a word as accepted by educated persons, "latent" is a poor term for phenomena that are usually there to be observed by the sociologist.

[23] Op. cit., esp. pp. 30–32.

[24] Pareto next goes into a discussion of maxima of utility, a question that in recent decades has received little or no attention at all. See especially §§2121–39.

It will be recalled that Merton isolated these two critical concepts through an enlightening discussion of an erroneous conception of functional analysis, which he labels the "postulate of indispensability." [25] Merton correctly argued that it is one thing to hold that a given function is indispensable, in which case we have a "functional prerequisite," but an entirely different thing to hold that a social form or action is indispensable. The principle of indispensability in the latter case is to be excluded in favor of the more tenable principle of "functional alternatives." Having made this essential clarification, however, Merton easily dismisses the problem with the statement that the functional prerequisite "remains one of the cloudiest and empirically most debatable concepts in functional theory." [26]

The question now arises as to whether this cloudy concept does not constitute an unnecessary problem for the functionalist. It would seem to me that the problem arose, to begin with, out of a persistent but largely fallacious biologic analogy utilized by many functional analysts. It is no secret that present-day functionalism is too narrowly identified with organismic-biological antecedents, ignoring roots in the mechanistic-physicalistic traditions. Thus it is that in seeking to prove the usefulness of a functional orientation in science, Merton's recourse was to the functionalism of the physiologist Cannon.[27] Again, the organismic tradition may partly explain Merton's excessive comparative emphasis on B. Malinowski and A. R. Radcliffe-Brown, though it must perforce puzzle the reader who can associate Merton with Harvard training at the time when Pareto was in great vogue at that university. Further, with reference to biological identification, one might explain as organismic obsession the recent contention by Martindale, cited above, that Pareto was an organicist and a transitional figure between organicism and sociological functionalism. In his brief excursion into Pareto's thought, Martindale failed to note that after sensitizing himself in no unsure terms to the dangers of using any type of analogy at all, Pareto preferred to use it, when necessary, "from mechanics." After all, his basic training was in the mathematical and physical sciences. Indeed, a careful reading of Pareto's discussion of the social system might by itself have sufficed to help Martindale avoid a most infelicitous assertion.

No matter. What is important now is the possibility that Pareto's physicalistic commitment is, more than biological organicism, equal

[25] Op. cit., pp. 32–37.   [26] Ibid., p. 52.   [27] Ibid., pp. 46–49.

to the needs of sociological analysis in this particular instance. It might be worthwhile if sociologists turned their attention to this question. Besides, we cannot for long neglect the criticisms of experts in methodology like Nagel, the philosopher of science, who in his brilliant discussion of functionalism in social science, has cogently argued that "the cognitive worth of functional explanations modeled on teleological explanations in physiology is . . . in the main very dubious." [28]

Functional Prerequisites. Would we do better with physicalistic models? It is certain that the concept of functional prerequisite (or the earlier bivalent postulate of indispensability) has been suggested to us by the concept of "survival" in biology. Now, as Nagel rightly argues,[29] in biology it is not only proper to speak of survival and "vital functions," but given the relatively simple nature and actual mortality of the organism, it is even empirically imperative. Yet what is there in the social system, or any unit therein, that corresponds to the vital function of "respiration," for instance, as a defining attribute of aliveness in the biological organism? Take away respiration and the organism dies. But the same cannot be said of the social system with respect to any of its activities. The social alternatives appear to be very many; societies do not literally die out—or only very rarely—but rather change their organization.

As has been justly argued on too many occasions to be cited here, the concept of functional prerequisite in social science would unavoidably lead us to status-quo ideologies and to empty tautologies or logically trivial theses. For instance, in discussing certain alleged prerequisites, the most we might be able to say is that in order to survive, a society needs some form of religion, some form of family, some form of government. But what theoretical value can such expressions have? What do they tell us about the great variability of social forms in time and space? With respect to government, for instance, the theoretically critical and fertile questions would rather seem to be in the nature of the following: In what way and in what measure does a given form of government contribute to the maintenance or achievement of a stated approximate condition (say, equality of social opportunities) in a given society? What mechanisms impinge on that form of government, on the stated condition, and on various other forms and processes involved in the larger social system? Pareto's physicalistic model leads him precisely in such directions.

[28] Op. cit., pp. 534–35.   [29] Ibid., pp. 527–30.

There is no room in his sociology for the concept of functional prerequisite, and his functionalism is couched in manifestly dynamic terms. For instance, he defines the social system as being characterized by a tendency to maintain a certain state and argues that if we intend to reason at all strictly, our first obligation is to fix upon the state in which we are choosing to consider the social system, which is constantly changing in form ($2067).

Now, if the system is examined in a determinate state, and this state is not viewed as an enduring one, it follows that the concept of functional prerequisite is totally irrelevant. The system changes in any case and assumes progressive "states X_1, X_2, X_3. . . ." The theoretically critical issue now becomes one of examining the mechanisms that alter the system from one state to another. Hence Pareto's preoccupation with elite circulation, which in the literature on him has generally been discussed as an isolated question, whereas in reality it is patently an expression of a functionalist analysis.

The physicalistic model has, therefore, served Pareto well.

As Nagel[30] again correctly suggests, it is hardly possible to overestimate the importance of imputing a certain function to a given variable relative to some particular state in some particular system. For in the absence of this simple requirement, all reasoning is without substantive content; any theoretical claims cannot be subjected to empirical control, since they are compatible with every conceivable matter of fact and with every outcome of empirical inquiries into actual society.

At least one other critical observation must now be made. Among all major functionalist concepts, that of "interdependence" must necessarily occupy a position in the forefront of functional analysis. For this concept is a definitional property of the concept of system itself. Yet of all known functionalists, it seems to me that none has taken the concept of interdependence as seriously as Pareto. Having isolated some of the critical elements impinging on the social system, and having defined the system as tending toward an X state of equilibrium while constantly changing in form, Pareto proceeds with the utmost logical rigor to an analysis of the modes in which the elements combine with each other in their operation on the social system. In brief, Pareto, unlike other functionalists, has not

[30] Op. cit. The failure to solve this problem is Nagel's major criticism of Merton in an otherwise favorable reference to him (p. 530). I submit that it is also the point of maximum difference between the positions of Pareto and Merton.

failed to raise the essential functionalist question: "What are the 'cycles of interdependence' among the constituents of the system?"

At least in part because of the failure to raise this fundamental question, many functionalists have been accused of inability to handle the analysis of social change. In response to such a reproach, Merton has suggested with characteristic keenness that the concept of "dysfunction" can well provide the basis of a proper sensitivity to problems of social change. Certainly the notion deserves serious consideration.

It would now appear, however, that social change in functional analysis can more fundamentally be dealt with through the hypothesis of interdependence in the social system. For if the units constituting the system are interdependent, the repercussions of movement in one unit combine with movements in other units, modifying these to some extent and thus producing chains of alterations. As for the very sources of change, they are many and are of both an endogenous and an exogenous nature. Later we shall note that Pareto focuses on two of these sources in particular: a gradual and cyclical alteration in the residues, and the internal conflict among the social classes which accompanies it.

The lesson of interdependence in the social system still remains to be learned in sociology, perhaps because sensitivity to it would require that assiduous, patient, and methodic application to social analysis that at our level of scientific maturity we do not yet possess. But such sensitivity would solve many theoretical problems. For instance, in an excellent study of social class and social change in Puerto Rico, Tumin unavoidably finds that Parsons' famous theory of social stratification is attuned to the ideal of a stable social system and is therefore not useful for making predictions about Puerto Rico, a society in transition.[31] I would submit that what is missing in Parsons' theory is the concept of interdependence among the elements that constitute it. Without this concept, and in the absence of a special, independent treatment of change in the theory, any changes in the social system studied obviously remain irrelevant, for they are extraneous to the theoretical construct.

Functional Alternatives. In returning now to the concept of functional alternative, let me say that unlike that of functional prerequisite, it plays a major role in Pareto's sociology. Pareto clearly

[31] Melvin Tumin, *Social Class and Social Change in Puerto Rico* (Princeton: Princeton University Press, 1961), p. 473.

recognized that the mechanisms impinging on a given state of equilibrium are many and in some cases equivalent. The point is brought
out most clearly in his discussion of the mechanisms which the ruling elite can control in its effort to delay its fall from power, though
in the long run this fall can never be entirely avoided. These mechanisms are consequently basic to both equilibrium maintenance and
to change in the social system:

1. The most effective such mechanism would be free and unhin-
dered circulation so that the ruling class would be continuously
replenished and invigorated with the ablest individuals available in
the society. Strictly speaking, however, this is a mechanism of self-
maintenance for the qualified and thus a very effective mechanism of
equilibrium maintenance in the system in general. But ruling elites
tend to resist circulation.

2. More practically, to defend and maintain itself the governing
class can resort to "diplomacy," fraud, corruption, and deception.
Specifically, the governing class finds ways to corrupt and to assimilate
"most of the individuals in the subject class who show those same
talents, are adept in those same arts, and might therefore become the
leaders of such plebeians as are disposed to use violence" (§2179).

3. Finally, the ruling class can use force to maintain its position.
Force must be understood to include such techniques as death,
persecution, imprisonment, exile, and ostracism.

Pareto's argument about the use of force in society provides a natural bridge between the two major topics of this essay, namely, the
question of functionalism and the dialectics of integration and coercion in society, which will now be discussed. As I see it, the two
topics correspond to the two fundamental concerns of present-day
analytical sociology. A treatment of the latter topic will also permit
me to dispose of a common, persistent, and absurd belief, most recently voiced by Martindale, that Pareto approved the use of the
most brutal force to crush innovation.

Consensus, Deception, and Coercion

in Pareto's Sociology

An old but fundamental question is still waiting to be answered by sociological theory: how do human societies cohere and endure? [32] So far, the search for a solution to this problem appears to have given rise to two major schools of thought, which allegedly yield two contrasting theories. In Dahrendorf's words: "One of these, the integration theory of society, conceives of social structure in terms of a functionally integrated system held in equilibrium by certain patterned and recurrent processes. The other one, the coercion theory of society, views social structure as a form of organization held together by force and constraint and reaching continuously beyond itself in the sense of producing within itself the forces that maintain it in an unending process of change." [33]

As Dahrendorf cogently argues—contrary to the claims of the respective advocates—neither of the two theories can be conceived as exclusively valid for all sociological problems and therefore for our major theoretical issue at hand. Certain sociological phenomena re-

[32] For a short sample of recent discussions, see: (1) Ralf Dahrendorf, "Toward a Theory of Social Conflict," *Journal of Conflict Resolution*, II (June 1958), 170–83; "Out of Utopia: Toward a Reorientation of Sociological Analysis," *American Journal of Sociology*, LXIV (September 1958), 115–27; *Class and Class Conflict in Industrial Society* (Stanford: Stanford University Press, 1959); "Conflict and Liberty: Some Remarks on the Social Structure of German Politics," *British Journal of Sociology*, XIV (September 1963), 197–211; (2) Lewis A. Coser, *The Functions of Social Conflict* (Gencoe, Ill.: The Free Press, 1956); (3) Florence R. Kluckhohn and Fred L. Strodbeck, *Variations in Value Orientations* (Evanston, Ill.: Row, Peterson, 1961); (4) Herman Turk, "Social Cohesion Through Variant Values," *American Sociological Review*, XXVIII (February 1963), 28–37; (5) Pierre L. van den Berghe, "Dialectic and Functionalism: Toward a Theoretical Synthesis," *American Sociological Review*, XXVIII (October 1963), pp. 695–705. Needless to add that the work of Talcott Parsons himself falls quite naturally within this general area, especially his *The Social System* (Glencoe, Ill.: The Free Press, 1951).

[33] Dahrendorf, *Class and Class Conflict in Industrial Society*, p. 159. More recently, van den Berghe (op. cit.) has convincingly argued about their complementary nature, but he has oddly attributed the two models to "fuctionalism" an "the Hegelian-Marxian dialectic" respectively.

quire one point of view; others need both theories for a more nearly complete explanation. Another way of saying this is that an adequate analysis of the social phenomenon must reflect the dialectics of stability and change, integration and conflict, function and motive force, consensus and coercion—all of which dualities characterize human societies.[34] According to Dahrendorf, however, "there is no such general model" in sociology.[35]

My own viewpoint is that when expressed in their complete terms, the two theories are not nearly so different as is generally believed. Indeed, the suggestion might be hazarded that within certain limitations inherent in the understandable lack of formal rigor characteristic of most available sociological theories, we have two general theories of society rather than none. Basically, the two existing ones differ only in the particular perspective they bring to bear on the dialectics of consensus and coercion as general properties of enduring social systems. Thus, one of them implicitly argues that the emphasis on consensus deserves a sort of sociological precedence because this property appears to neutralize the social differences and the concomitant conflicts inevitably arising in society; the other shifts the accent to conflict and coercion, both as major and ever-present realities of the society and as social processes that periodically steer a poorly integrated social system toward a better integrated state. Coercion and consensus are, therefore, fundamental to each perspective. But what may be reasonable to hold is that each of the two theories, as an instrument of analysis, is lacking in the "temperament" necessary to take into account some of the social phenomena deemed crucial by the other.

But are there in sociology variations of the two theories which on close scrutiny yield a general theory "temperamentally" neutral? I hope to demonstrate that to a considerable extent one such theory was in fact developed in Pareto's sociology. Indeed, Dahrendorf himself comes very close to making this discovery when, in referring to Pareto's treatment of elite circulation, he states that "if Pareto claims that history is 'a cemetery of aristocracies,' he leaves it open whether group conflicts or other forces caused the death of ruling elites." [36] We shall return to this point later.

[34] *Class and Class Conflict*, p. 163.   [35] Ibid., p. 164.   [36] Ibid., p. 198.

CONSENSUS AND COERCION VIA SOCIALITY

Pareto's synthesis of the two theories comes about in his discussion of "the use of force in society" in terms of "the residues of sociality." His argument is extensive and complex. Roughly, however, it is anchored to the position that a given degree of consensus in society is achieved for two major and complementary orders of reasons. One of these orders may be expressed in terms of mechanisms of sociality that are either institutionalized or invented ad hoc by certain individuals or groups in a society. The other order of reasons may be conceived in terms of responses, based on socially conditioned "sentiments," that the individual gives to the mechanisms of sociality.

Thus, in the former case we have such mechanisms as systems of transcendental ends, "natural law," and other "theories transcending experience" (§§401–463) which, in some cases at least, help subject individual differences to an indisputable arbitration. Or we may have certain political ideologies invented by ruling classes in order to achieve social stability, to legitimate their authority, to perpetuate it, or otherwise to practice fraud on the masses, as when a ruling oligarchy teaches that insurrection is illegitimate because a "state of law" exists (§2182).

In the latter case certain deep-lying sentiments, wishes, or values predispose the individual in a way that facilitates the operation of the former. Among these may be a "need of group approbation" (§§1160–62), whereby the individual is impelled to engage in conduct not inimical to the sentiments and needs of others, and a "neophobia" (§§1130–32) which, as "a sentiment of hostility to innovations that are calculated to disturb uniformities," tends to reinforce common sentiments and existing consensus. It is such inclinations of the individual toward the social situation that provide the materia prima cementing the social fabric together. As Pareto argues, in the last analysis societies survive because, in the majority of their members there are sentiments alive and vigorous that correspond to the residues of sociality (§2170), namely, certain predispositions for association and cooperation with others, whether it be for purposes of mere amusement, or religious, political, or artistic expression, or individual advantage, or what have you (§1114).

Pareto summarizes this theoretical position by introducing a tend-

ency toward uniformity in the individual, which in his classification
of the residues then becomes a "need of uniformity" (§§1115–32).
And this is the critical point at which the notion of conflict (and
eventually coercion) comes in, for societies are essentially heterogeneous, meaning among other things that the need of uniformity
is not equally strong in all members of a society. According to Pareto,
"that fact has two interesting consequences which stand in apparent
contradiction, one of them threatening the dissolution of a society,
the other making for its progress in civilization. What at bottom is
there is continuous movement, but it is a movement that may
progress in almost any direction" (§2170).

More practically, the differential potency of the sentiments of uniformity will have, as a consequence, the appearance of "two theologies," "one of which will glorify the immobility of one or another
uniformity, real or imaginary, the other of which will glorify movement, progress, in one direction or another" (§2173). The two theologies must, or course, be viewed as ideal types. In reality human
societies are highly heterogeneous, and differences in uniformity may
vary according to numerous groupings of individuals, so that in a
given society there are not merely "two centers of similarity," but "a
number of centers." The result is potential, and oftentimes real, conflict between the different "sets," some trying to extend their own
particular uniformity to others (§1116).

We are still at a high level of abstraction. In the concrete, the
actual processes that yield social conflict are numerous. Pareto discusses two in some detail. One of them concerns social circulation,
which may be viewed as competition for a very scarce and desirable
good, namely the political authority and the social perquisites that
this entails. This type of conflict is continual, but basically it arises
only among the politically active elite, that is, those relatively few individuals in the society who, whether already in positions of political
administration or seeking to join them, are distinguished from the
masses, at least early in their careers, by their exceptional talent. The
masses themselves are not strangers to this form of conflict; their participation in it, however, is based less on political interest and more
on repulsion caused by the discordant sentiments of their ruling class
at a particular time.

The other major area of social conflict is the economic sphere. To
better understand this, we must refer back to the political question.
The political conflict just mentioned generally arises between two

classes of individuals, that is, the "foxes" and the "lions," characterized respectively by the sentiments of "combinations" and those of "group-persistence." With the former are associated scheming, inventiveness, and innovation; with the latter are associated directness, traditionalism, and stability. The economic sphere of society has counterparts to those two classes of individuals, which here become "speculators" and "rentiers." The conflict between these generally lies in the fact that the rentiers are cautious savers rather than enterprising capitalists. Thus they tend to react against economic extravagance, scheming, and sometimes exploitation on the part of the speculators. Such reaction frequently takes the form of an alliance with the political lions against the foxes, which latter in general coincide with and are favorable to the rising of the speculators.

Now as concerns the use of force: whatever the source or the cause of conflict, almost invariably the use of force is concomitant with its rise, "for force is used by those who wish to preserve certain uniformities and by those who wish to overstep them; and the violence of the ones stands in contrast and in conflict with the violence of the others" ($2174—italics added). If there are differences in the readiness with which force is used under given circumstances, they are due to the differential intensity of the "faith" with which uniformities are held.

This particular position regarding the universality of coercion brings us to an important distinction: conformity by the individual can be voluntary as well as enforced. The human being, as Pareto argues, not only imitates to become like others; he wants others to do likewise. The reason for this enforced conformity must be found with reference to the sentiments of the "integrity of the individual and his appurtenances" ($$1207–1323). More specifically, when a person departs from the common standards, his conduct seems to jar and produces a sense of discomfort in the persons associated with him. "An effort is made to eliminate the jar, now by persuasion, more often by censure, more often still by force" ($1126).

We can already notice that the basic forces of integration and consensus are also the ultimate causes of conflict and coercion. There is, in fact, a reciprocal relationship between consensus and coercion that might be expressed in the following terms: just as the requirement of uniformity (and thus consensus) is the ultimate cause of coercion, so the use of force is, in some unspecified degree and for an unspecified period of time, also the cause of consensus; for coercion, as a response to the need of uniformity, tends to strengthen conformity and therefore integration, consensus, and stability in the society.

In a recent critique of functionalism (which again excludes Pareto's sociology) this basic point is expressed thus: "In a nutshell my argument is that, while societies do indeed show a tendency towards stability, equilibrium, and consensus, they simultaneously generate within themselves the opposites of these." [37]

Pareto's basic model is of a very general nature, but it was intended to be widely applicable in the analysis of the social phenomenon. As far as his own concrete application of it is concerned, however, he sought to simplify his job by focusing on the interaction between two major social classes in society, namely, the ruling class and the governed class.[38] According to Pareto, it is the relations between these two classes that to a large extent articulate the mode of social organization and the degree of social cohesion or disintegration in society. Consequently, the concrete discussion of the relationship between social order on the one hand and consensus and coercion on the other is presented by Pareto in terms of the actions and interactions of these two classes.

In general, it can be said that the ruling and the subject classes stand toward each other "very much as two nations respectively alien" (§2227). The fundamental reason for such conflict lies in their different value orientations. To be sure, it often happens that when a ruling class first seizes the reigns of government, it is characterized by those same values and that same fervor that characterize the masses of the governed class. That is to say, at this point the ruling class is to a very large extent truly representative of the governed class. But eventually "The individual comes to prevail, and by far, over family, community, nation. Material interests and interests of the present or a near future come to prevail over the ideal interests of community or nation and interests of the distant future. The impulse is to enjoy the present without too much thought for the morrow" (§2178).

What is happening is that the sentiments of group-persistence are giving way to the sentiments of combinations, leading away from value integration toward compromising, scheming, and lack of social control. The reasons are various, but four are of fundamental im-

[37] van den Berghe, pp. 696–97.
[38] This division bears great resemblance to Dahrendorf's own dichotomous division in terms of relation to the authority structure of society.

portance: (1) the maintenance of power becomes an end in itself, a good to maintain at all costs; (2) this tendency is in turn supported by the habit, often only recently acquired, of living a plush life at public expense,[39] (3) the use of force becomes increasingly difficult because of the potential threat of strong reaction by the governed class, as well as a natural revulsion to using force against those who previously were faithful supporters and followers; (4) the governed masses have heterogeneous "appetites," and are likely to make demands not consonant with collective utilities.

But the matter of using force is particularly critical: Pareto argues that when a ruling class is unwilling or unable to use force, it encourages anarchic action in the general population. That is, whenever the influence of public authority declines, there grow up within the state smaller states and societies threatening the citizen with private vendettas, summary justice, and various other forms of antisocial actions. Indeed, when a ruling class divests itself completely of the sentiments of group-persistence (and therefore of the use of force), it reaches the point where it is unable to protect from external threats the citizens that it allegedly represents. In other words, in the extreme case, Pareto's argument is that the failure to use a certain degree of force (the problem of specifying this remains unsolved) results in the failure of the system itself, very frequently through the use of force by hostile societies. In such cases, it often happens that the subject class yields the faith and the resolve to save itself and the society by using force against and overthrowing its governing class. But not always, for many are the societies that have not reacted adjustively to external threats. In most cases, however, "the differences in temperament" and interests between the ruling class and the governed class become so great that the subject class becomes forceful and intransigent in its opposition to its ruling class, and revolution occurs. Revolution, therefore, may be thought of as a process through which a period of accumulated maladjustment or disintegration in the social system is brought to an end and a new state of equilibrium and relative integration is initiated.

The dialectics of stability and change, consensus and coercion could not be clearer. What needs to be pointed out, perhaps, is a very slight tendency on Pareto's part toward the coercion theory. According to Pareto, a social order inevitably deteriorates—for one

[39] For vivid accounts of "corruption" in his own country, see Pareto's *The Ruling Class in Italy Before 1900* (New York: S. F. Vanni, 1950), esp. pp. 11–82.

set of reasons or another—to the point where its value system is torn apart, as it were, and then put back together by acts of violence which express the growing need of value integration or uniformity in the society. Thus Pareto shared much of Marxist theory, at least with respect to the role of conflict as an endogenous cause of social change and social reintegration. What he did not share, as a skeptic and a realistic observer of history and human nature, was Marx's excessively rationalistic prediction of a definitive resolution of conflict through victory by the masses. For Pareto, "it is always an oligarchy that governs," and "history is a graveyard of aristocracies." A ruling class comes to power, inevitably it degenerates or is corrupted, and finally it disappears to make way for another that will do likewise.

At this point let me go back to the question that opened the present discussion and suggest that, given Pareto's practical focus on social circulation, the question of "what holds society together" has precious little meaning for him. Or better still, the question is theoretically sterile, for societies always cohere, more or less at different times. The sentiments of uniformity and other mechanisms of social integration are always at work in some degree. What happens in reality is that social cohesion expresses itself in a process of continual conflict coupled with continual, and sometimes abrupt and radical, social transformation. The critical question for Pareto must therefore be couched in somewhat different terms, namely: what are the particular processes, as well as their duration and direction, that gnaw at cohesion in the society to the point where strong reactions periodically occur and new major states of equilibrium or social cohesion are achieved in the social system?

It should now be noted that Pareto's own analysis of social change in terms of value changes in the two major classes of society (and particularly the ruling class) may be fundamental to social reality, but it grossly oversimplifies it. His theory, therefore, must be viewed as a rough heuristic device which in the phenomenon of social circulation singles out a major perspective at social change, at the same time that it invites attention to the concrete social processes that in a given society and in a given period initiate, bear, and bring to an end an equilibrium cycle.

If this consideration is valid, it must ultimately mean also that Pareto has no real theory of social change. I would hold that his observations about cycles of change along the axis of the authority structure was intended on the one hand as a program of basic premises for a more complete theory of social change to come, and on the other hand it was intended as a functionalist illustration of the reciprocal effects between two major classes of residues and between these and other elements constituting the system. No doubt Pareto was aware that his "cyclical theory" did not focus on all, or even the major, aspects of social change. It must be noted that he made an important distinction between substance and form in the social phenomenon, and the notion of cycle applies only to the substance of authority in society—and then only in a particular area of it: the political system. A change in the value substance of the society brings about a change in authority distribution (elite circulation) but usually no basic change in social structure. Pareto, however, recognized that from society to society, and less often from time to time within the same society, governments also change in their form (§§2237–78).

DECEPTION: A THIRD DIMENSION

So far, in answering our leading question I have been concerned mainly with the interrelationship between consensus and coercion. I must now suggest that there is a third dimension to a more nearly complete answer to that query. This might be simply expressed with the term "deception," covering such others as fraud, trickery, chicanery, cunning, ruse, and manipulation. The sociological literature is rich in the analysis of such phenomena. Pareto's own emphasis on this concept is colorfully evidenced by his recalling the legend of the slaying of the brave Xanthus, king of the Boeotians, by the deceitful Melanthus, king of the Athenians. In this connection he rightly observes that "rare the mythological or historical narrative of antiquity in which treachery does not play some part . . ." (§1927). The same no doubt could be said of modern times: the point need not be elaborated; it is enough to keep one's ears open during political elections—to mention but one major case.

As regards Pareto's own treatment of deception, in its most relevant form it can be found in his discussion, presented above, of mechanisms available to the ruling class for defending its position. To delay its fall, instead of using force the governing class sometimes "bows its head under the threat of violence, but it surrenders only in appearances, trying to turn the flank of the obstacle it cannot demolish in frontal attack" (§2178). That is to say, the governing class finds ways to corrupt and to assimilate most of those in the subject class who might become leaders of revolt.

The question now arises as to whether deception is sufficiently different from the other two major concepts (coercion and consensus) to warrant a separate discussion of it. If such difference exists, then its widespread existence in society would seem to warrant its inclusion as a major component of a general theory of society. On close scrutiny it appears that all forms of coercion, whether physical punishment, persecution, imprisonment, exile, ostracism, threats, or something else, involve actions actually or potentially perpetrated against individuals or groups and intended to provoke immediate pain or discomfort in the coerced, who in turn cannot help but be aware of the application of coercion against them. Consensus, on the other hand, would seem to refer to a state of mutual and peaceful agreement—contractual or traditional—between some parties interacting about a common goal or a commonly relevant social fact. Deception fits neither of these two phenomena. It is not coercion, inasmuch as a deceptive act is sometimes expressed in the form of "sweet hypocrisy" which arouses a pleased, grateful, or otherwise favorable response on the part of the deceived. Similarly, it is not consensus, because the deceiver does in fact not abide by the agreement or standards of conduct that the deceived believes to be reciprocally valid. Indeed, deception may be viewed as a technique of achieving consensus calculated to be advantageous to one party at the expense of another. It seems, therefore, that the types of phenomena isolated with the concepts of "consensus," "deception," and "coercion" belong to three major and separate orders of reality, so that they should be kept analytically distinct in the construction of a general theory of sociological analysis.

COMMENTS

In the light of the above discussion it may be reasonable to conclude that a synthetic theory of the sort called for by Dahrendorf is to a considerable extent available in the sociology of Vilfredo Pareto. Such a theory views society as a social system tending toward equilibrium yet "constantly changing in form." It hypothesizes an interdependence and an integration of parts within a basic context of conflict of interests. It postulates a requirement of uniformity in the individual which, because of differential adherence to it, leads to fundamental and general coercion; but coercion sometimes yields consensus, just as the need for consensus yields its opposite. The theory takes into account social change of both endogenous and exogenous origins. Finally, the theory hypothesizes a certain degree of stability, but at the same time it postulates a precondition of it in class circulation, which in turn may occur because of conflict and revolution as well as various other factors, among which is the ability of the ruling class temporarily to weaken the opposition by defrauding it of those elements that could best organize it into a revolution. Consensus, deception, and coercion appear, therefore, to be complementary forces in the cohesion of society.

It follows that it is not exact, as Dahrendorf has suggested, that Pareto leaves open the question whether group conflicts or other forces cause the death of ruling elites. Pareto argues that the explanation of their fall is to be found by reference to heterogenous forces, including internal degeneration, rational and fraudulent circulation, economic conflict, revolution by the governed class, and destruction at the hand of a hostile and alien society. In turn, ruling elites can at least delay their fall by practicing a popular "faith," by admitting into their ranks some of the highly competent individuals who are elite among the masses, by using fraud and deception, and by using force. Some causes of fall are, therefore, also the same causes of authority maintenance. The apparent paradox is explained by the fact that the fall is in the long run inevitable, which simply means that stability and instability are inseparable characteristics of the social system.

Analogously, if Pareto can justly be considered a full-fledged functionalist, as I have argued, then the argument occasionally heard that functionalists are "slanted" toward the consensus and stability theory of society may have to be re-examined.[40] As we have seen, in functionalist Pareto there is in fact a slight propensity toward the coercion theory, in the sense that whereas he views consensus as a basic requirement in individual behavior, he also considers coercion an inevitable process that makes consensus possible.

Again, in view of the above discussion it seems particularly odd to read in a recent paper that

. . . a dynamic equilibrium model cannot account for the irreducible facts that:

[40] See, for instance, van den Berghe, p. 698.

1) reaction to extra-systemic change is not always adjustive,
2) social systems can, for long periods, go through a vicious circle of ever deepening malintegration,
3) change can be revolutionary, i.e., both sudden and profound,
4) the social structure itself generates change through internal conflicts and contradictions.[41]

I believe the answer to these assertions has been amply given in our discussion of Pareto, in whose sociology few readers have failed to recognize a dynamic equilibrium theory.

Let it be noted now that it is not my intention to prove that Pareto's sociology contains a fully developed general theory of sociological analysis. Much work no doubt remains to be done, and it is not even unlikely that a close look at the available literature would reveal greater development in other scholars before and since Pareto. What I have endeavored to do is to demonstrate that Pareto's theory ties together many of the elements of two other available theories, correcting in part their respective inadequacies. This statement made by Pareto in connection with his discussion of forms of government in society may in itself suffice to give a concrete idea of the direction and temper of Pareto's sociological analysis: "Ignoring exceptions, which are few in number and of short duration, one finds everywhere a governing class of relatively few individuals that keeps itself in power partly by force and partly by the consent of the subject class, which is much more populous. The differences lie principally, as regards substance, in the relative proportions of force and consent; and as regards forms, in the manners in which the force is used and the consent obtained" (§2244).

Biographical Note

Vilfredo Pareto was born the son of an Italian exile in Paris on July 15, 1848, and died at Céligny, Switzerland, on August 19, 1923. At the age of twenty-two he earned a degree in engineering from the celebrated Polytechnic Institute in Turin, Italy, after defending a thesis on "the index functions of equilibrium in solid bodies." In the next ten years he was first a consulting engineer for the Italian railways and then general superintendent of three iron mines owned by

[41] Ibid., pp. 697–98.

the Banca Nazionale of Florence. While he was in this post, Pareto began to interest himself seriously in economic questions. Eventually he made a number of important contributions to economics which in 1894 won for him the chair of political economy at Lausanne upon nomination by the great Swiss economist Leon Walras, just then retiring from that post.

Throughout his life, Pareto was an avid reader in various other disciplines, principally history, philosophy, and the classics. While this vast scholarship, coupled with his scientific genius, led him to discover the preponderant influence of non-logical reasoning in human conduct, his study of economics directed his attention (as has also happened with many other great sociologists) to the need for a more encompassing social discipline than economics to study society in its general form.

Pareto's Writings

Pareto was a prolific writer, and his ideas are found in a very large body of books, articles, and letters. The Treatise on General Sociology, first published in Italian in 1916, is Pareto's major sociological work and the source of all the quotations and selections included in the present volume. They are reprinted, with the permission of the Pareto Fund, from the two-volume English translation by Andrew Bongiorno and Arthur Livingston, entitled The Mind and Society.[42] A few of Pareto's other well-known writings are:

Cours d'économie politique. 2 vols. Lausanne: Rouge, 1896–97.
Les Systèmes socialistes. Paris: Giard et Brière, 1902.
Manuale d'Economia politica. Milan: Società Editrice Libraria, 1906.
Fatti e Teorie. Florence: Vallecchi, 1920.
Trasformazione della Democrazia. Milan: Corbaccio, 1921.
Lettere a Maffeo Pantaleoni, ed. Gabriele DeRosa. 3 vols. Rome: Banca Nazionale del Lavoro, 1960.

[42] Edited by Arthur Livingston (New York: Dover Publications, Inc., 1963).

Non-Logical Action

7.* Current in any given group of people are a number of propositions, descriptive, preceptive, or otherwise. For example: "Youth lacks discretion." "Covet not thy neighbour's goods, nor thy neighbour's wife." "Love thy neighbour as thyself." "Learn to save if you would not one day be in need." Such propositions, combined by logical or pseudo-logical nexuses and amplified with factual narrations of various sorts, constitute theories, theologies, cosmogonies, systems of metaphysics, and so on. Viewed from the outside without regard to any intrinsic merit with which they may be credited by faith, all such propositions and theories are experimental facts, and as experimental facts we are here obliged to consider and examine them.

8. That examination is very useful to sociology; for the image of social activity is stamped on the majority of such propositions and theories, and often it is through them alone that we manage to gain some knowledge of the forces which are at work in society—that is, of the tendencies and inclinations [sentiments] of human beings.

. . . . .

130. . . . We . . . are to consider propositions and theories under their *objective* and their *subjective aspects,* and also from the standpoint of their individual or social *utility.* . . .

14. . . . Given the proposition A = B, we must answer the following questions:

1. *Objective aspect.* Is the proposition in accord with experience, or is it not?

2. *Subjective aspect.* Why do certain individuals assert that A = B? And why do other individuals believe that A = B?

* It is the custom to refer to any part of Pareto's *Treatise* by its section number rather than by page number.—J.L.

36

3. *Aspect of utility.* What advantage (or disadvantage) do the sentiments reflected by the proposition $A = B$ have for the person who states it, and for the person who accepts it? What advantage (or disadvantage) does the theory itself have for the person who puts it forward, and for the person who accepts it? . . .

. . . We shall see, as we proceed with our experimental research . . . that the following cases are of frequent occurrence in social matters:

a. Propositions in accord with experience that are asserted and accepted because of their accord with sentiments, the latter being now beneficial, now detrimental, to individuals or society

b. Propositions in accord with experience that are rejected because they are not in accord with sentiments, and which, if accepted, would be detrimental to society

c. Propositions not in accord with experience that are asserted and accepted because of their accord with sentiments, the latter being beneficial, oftentimes exceedingly so, to individuals or society

d. Propositions not in accord with experience that are asserted and accepted because of their accord with sentiments, and which are beneficial to certain individuals, detrimental to others, and now beneficial, now detrimental, to society.

. . . . .

149. Every social phenomenon may be considered under two aspects: as it is in reality, and as it presents itself to the mind of this or that human being. The first aspect we shall call *objective*, the second *subjective*.† Such a division is necessary, for we cannot put in one same class the operations performed by a chemist in his laboratory and the operations performed by a person practising magic; the conduct of Greek sailors in plying their oars to drive their ship over the water and the sacrifices they offered to Poseidon to make sure of a safe and rapid voyage. . . .

We must not be misled by the names we give to the two classes. In reality both are subjective, for all human knowledge is subjective. They are to be distinguished not so much by any difference in nature as in view of the greater or lesser fund of factual knowledge that we ourselves have. We know, or think we know, that sacrifices to Poseidon have no effect whatsoever upon a voyage. We therefore distinguish

† A discussion of objective and subjective aspects now follows. The aspect of utility is very closely linked to Pareto's discussion of the social system and is taken up in that connection.—J.L.

them from other acts which (to our best knowledge, at least) are
capable of having such effect. If at some future time we were to discover that we have been mistaken, that sacrifices to Poseidon are very
influential in securing a favourable voyage, we should have to re-
classify them with actions capable of such influence. . . .

150. There are actions that use means appropriate to ends and
which logically link means with ends. There are other actions in
which those traits are missing. The two sorts of conduct are very
different according as they are considered under their objective or
their subjective aspect. From the subjective point of view nearly all
human actions belong to the logical class. In the eyes of the Greek
mariners sacrifices to Poseidon and rowing with oars were equally
logical means of navigation. To avoid verbosities which could only
prove annoying, we had better give names to these types of conduct.
Suppose we apply the term *logical actions* to actions that logically
conjoin means to ends not only from the standpoint of the subject
performing them, but from the standpoint of other persons who have
a more extensive knowledge—in other words, to actions that are logical both subjectively and objectively in the sense just explained.
Other actions we shall call *non-logical* (by no means the same as
"illogical"). This latter class we shall subdivide into a number of
varieties.

151. A synoptic picture of the classification will prove useful:

GENERA AND SPECIES   HAVE THE ACTIONS LOGICAL ENDS AND PURPOSES:

Objectively?   Subjectively?

CLASS I: LOGICAL ACTIONS

(The objective end and the subjective purpose are identical.)

Yes   Yes

CLASS II: NON-LOGICAL ACTIONS

(The objective end differs from the subjective purpose.)

Genus 1	No	No
Genus 2	No	Yes
Genus 3	Yes	No
Genus 4	Yes	Yes

SPECIES OF THE GENERA 3 AND 4

3α, 4α   The objective end would be accepted by the subject
           if he knew it.
3β, 4β   The objective end would be rejected by the subject
           if he knew it.

The ends and purposes here in question are immediate ends and
purposes. We choose to disregard the indirect. The objective end is
a real one, located within the field of observation and experience,
and not an imaginary end, located outside that field. An imaginary
end may, on the other hand, constitute a subjective purpose.

152. Logical actions are very numerous among civilized peoples.
Actions connected with the arts and sciences belong to that class, at
least for artists and scientists. For those who physically perform them
in mere execution of orders from superiors, there may be among
them non-logical actions of our II-4 type. The actions dealt with
in political economy also belong in very great part in the class of
logical actions. In the same class must be located, further, a certain
number of actions connected with military, political, legal, and
similar activities.

153. So at the very first glance induction leads to the discovery
that non-logical actions play an important part in society. Let us
therefore proceed with our examination of them.

154. . . . Genera 1 and 3, which have no subjective purpose, are
of scant importance to the human race. Human beings have a very
conspicuous tendency to paint a varnish of logic over their conduct.
Nearly all human actions therefore work their way into genera 2
and 4. Many actions performed in deference to courtesy and custom
might be put in genus 1. But very very often people give some
reason or other to justify such conduct, and that transfers it to genus
2. Ignoring the indirect motive involved in the fact that a person
violating common usages incurs criticism and dislike, we might find
a certain number of actions to place in genera 1 and 3.

Says Hesiod: "Do not make water at the mouth of a river empty-
ing into the sea, nor into a spring. You must avoid that. Do not
lighten your bowels there, for it is not good to do so." The precept
not to befoul rivers at their mouths belongs to genus 1. No objective or subjective end or purpose is apparent in the avoidance of such
pollution. The precept not to befoul drinking-water belongs to genus

3. It has an objective purpose that Hesiod may not have known, but which is familiar to moderns: to prevent contagion from certain diseases.

It is probable that not a few actions of genera 1 and 3 are common among savages and primitive peoples. But travellers are bent on learning at all costs the reasons for the conduct they observe. So in one way or another they finally obtain answers that transfer the conduct to genera 2 and 4.

.   .   .   .   .

160. . . . Operations in magic when unattended by other actions belong to genus 2. The sacrifices of the Greeks and Romans have to be classed in the same genus—at least after those peoples lost faith in the reality of their gods. Hesiod, Opera et dies, vv. 735-39, warns against crossing a river without first washing one's hands in it and uttering a prayer. That would be an action of genus 1. But he adds that the gods punish anyone who crosses a river without so washing his hands. That makes it an action of genus 2.

.   .   .   .   .

Most acts of public policy based on tradition or on presumed missions of peoples or individuals belong to genus 4. William I, King of Prussia, and Napoleon III, Emperor of the French, both considered themselves "men of destiny." But William I thought his mission lay in promoting the welfare and greatness of his country, Louis Napoleon believed himself destined to achieve the happiness of mankind. William's policies were of the 4a type; Napoleon's, of the 4β.

.   .   .   .   .

161. Logical actions are at least in large part results of processes of reasoning. Non-logical actions originate chiefly in definite psychic states, sentiments, subconscious feelings, and the like. It is the province of psychology to investigate such psychic states. Here we start with them as data of fact, without going beyond that.

.   .   .   .   .

261. Rare the writer who fails to take any account of non-logical conduct whatever; but generally the interest is in certain natural inclinations of temperament, which, willynilly, the writer has to credit to human beings. But the eclipse of logic is of short duration —driven off at one point, it reappears at some other. The rôle of temperament is reduced to lowest terms, and it is assumed that

people draw logical inferences from it and act in accordance with them.

262. So much for the general situation. But in the particular, theorists have another very powerful motive for preferring to think of non-logical conduct as logical. If we assume that certain conduct is logical, it is much easier to formulate a theory about it than it is when we take it as non-logical. We all have handy in our minds the tool for producing logical inferences, and nothing else is needed. Whereas in order to organize a theory of non-logical conduct we have to consider hosts and hosts of facts, ever extending the scope of our researches in space and in time, and ever standing on our guard lest we be led into error by imperfect documents. In short, for the person who would frame such a theory, it is a long and difficult task to find outside himself materials that his mind supplied directly with the aid of mere logic when he was dealing with logical conduct.

263. If the science of political economy has advanced much further than sociology, that is chiefly because it deals with logical conduct. . . .

264. Other considerations tend to keep thinkers from the field of non-logical conduct and carry them over into the field of the logical. Most scholars are not satisfied with discovering what is. They are anxious to know, and even more anxious to explain to others, what ought to be. In that sort of research, logic reigns supreme; and so the moment they catch sight of conduct that is non-logical, instead of going ahead along that road they turn aside, often seem to forget its existence, at any rate generally ignore it, and beat the well-worn path that leads to logical conduct.

265. Some writers likewise rid themselves of non-logical actions by regarding them—often without saying as much explicitly—as scandalous things, or at least as irrelevant things, which should have no place in a well-ordered society. They think of them as "superstitions" that ought to be extirpated by the exercise of intelligence. Nobody, in practice, acts on the assumption that the physical and the moral constitution of an individual do not have at least some small share in determining his behavior. But when it comes to framing a theory, it is held that the human being ought to act rationally, and writers deliberately close their minds to things that the experience of every day holds up before their eyes.

266. The imperfection of ordinary language from the scientific

standpoint also contributes to the wide-spread resort to logical interpretations of non-logical conduct.

267. It plays no small part in the common misapprehension whereby two phenomena are placed in a relationship of cause and effect for the simple reason that they are found in company. . . .

Let C, as in Figure 1, stand for a belief; D, for certain behaviour. Instead of saying simply, "Some people do D and believe C," ordinary speech goes farther and says, "Some people do D because

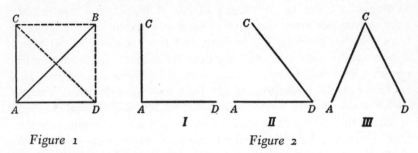

Figure 1   Figure 2

they believe C." Taken strictly, that proposition is often false. Less often false is the proposition, "Some people believe C because they do D." But there are still many occasions when all that we can say is, "Some men do D and believe C."

In the proposition, "Some people do D because they believe C," the logical strictness of the term "because" can be so attenuated that no relationship of cause and effect is set up between C and D. We can then say, "We may assume that certain people do D because they have a belief C which expresses sentiments that impel them to do D"; that is because . . . they have a psychic state A that is expressed by C. In such a form the proposition closely approximates the truth. . . .

268. Figure 1 can be broken up into three others (Figure 2).

I. The psychic state A produces the belief C and the conduct D, there being no direct relation between C and D. That is the situation in the proposition, "People do D and believe C."

II. The psychic state A gives rise to the conduct D, and they both produce the belief C. That is the situation in the second proposition, "People believe C because they do D."

III. The psychic state A gives rise to the belief C, which produces the behaviour D. That is the situation in the proposition, "People do D because they believe C."

269. Although case III is not the only case, nor even the most frequent case, people are inclined to regard it as general and to merge with it cases I and II to which they preferably attribute little or no importance. Ordinary language, with its lack of exactness, encourages the error, because a person may state case III explicitly and be unconsciously thinking meantime of cases I and II. It often happens, besides, that we get mixtures of the three cases in varying proportions.

270. Aristotle opens his *Politics*, I, 1, 1 (Rackham, p. 3), with the statement: "Seeing that every city is a society (Rackham, "partnership") and that every society (partnership) is constituted to the end of some good (for all men work to achieve what to them seems good) it is manifest that all societies (partnerships) seek some good." Here we stand altogether in the domain of logic: with a deliberate purpose—the purpose of achieving a certain good—human beings have constituted a society that is called a city. It would seem as though Aristotle were on the point of going off into the absurdities of the "social contract"! But not so. He at once changes tack, and the principle he has stated he will use to determine what a city *ought* to be rather than what it actually is.

271. The moment Aristotle has announced his principle—an association for purposes of mutual advantage—he tosses it aside and gives an altogether different account of the origin of society. First he notes the necessity of a union between the sexes, and soundly remarks that "that does not take place of deliberate choice"; wherewith, evidently, we enter the domain of non-logical conduct. He continues: "Nature has created certain individuals to command and others to obey." Among the Greeks Nature has so distinguished women and slaves. Not so among the Barbarians, for among the Barbarians, Nature has not appointed any individuals to command. We are still, therefore, in the domain of non-logical conduct; nor do we leave it when Aristotle explains that the two associations of master and slave, husband and wife, are the foundations of the family, that the village is constituted by several families, and that several villages form a state; nor when, finally, he concludes with the explicit declaration that "Every city, therefore, like the original associations, comes of Nature." One could not allude to non-logical actions in clearer terms.

272. But, alas, if the city comes of Nature, it does not come of the deliberate will of citizens who get together for the purpose of

achieving a certain advantage! There is an inconsistency between the principle first posited and the conclusion reached. Just how Aristotle fell into it we cannot know, but to accomplish that feat for oneself, one may proceed in the following fashion: First centre exclusively on the idea of "city," or "state." It will then be easy to connect city, or state, with the idea of "association," and then to connect association with the idea of *deliberate* association. So we get the first principle. But now think, in the second place, of the many many facts observable in a city or a state—the family, masters and slaves, and so on. Deliberate purpose will not fit in with those things very well. They suggest rather the notion of something that develops naturally. And so we get Aristotle's second description.

273. He gets rid of the contradiction by metaphysics, which never withholds its aid in these desperate cases. Recognizing non-logical conduct, he says, I, 1, 12 (Rackham, pp. 11–13): "It is therefore manifest that the city is a product of Nature and is superior (prior) to man (to the individual). From Nature accordingly comes the tendency (an impulse) in all men toward such association. Therefore the man who first founded one was the cause of a very great good." So then, there is the inclination imparted by Nature; but it is further necessary that a man found the city. So a logical action is grafted upon the non-logical action; and there is no help for that, for, says Aristotle, Nature does nothing in vain. Our best thanks, therefore, to that estimable demoiselle for so neatly rescuing a philosopher from a predicament!

. . . . .

798. Our detailed examination of one theory or another has . . . led to our perceiving that theories in the concrete may be divided into at least two elements, one of which is much more stable than the other. We say, accordingly, that in concrete theories, which we shall designate as c, there are, besides factual data, two principal elements (or parts); a substantial element (part), which we shall designate as a, and a contingent element (part), on the whole fairly variable, which we shall designate as b.

The element a directly corresponds to non-logical conduct; it is the expression of certain sentiments. The element b is the manifestation of the need of logic that the human being feels. It also partially corresponds to sentiments, to non-logical conduct, but it clothes them with logical or pseudo-logical reasonings. The element a is the *principle* existing in the mind of the human being; the element *b* is the explanation (or explanations) of that principle, the inference (or inferences) that he draws from it.

799. There is, for example, a principle, or if you prefer, a sentiment, in virtue of which certain numbers are deemed worthy of veneration: it is the chief element, *a*. . . . But the human being is not satisfied with merely associating sentiments of veneration with numbers; he also wants to "explain" how that comes about, to "demonstrate" that in doing what he does he is prompted by force of logic. So the element *b* enters in, and we get various "explanations," various "demonstrations," as to why certain numbers are sacred. There is in the human being a sentiment that restrains him from discarding old beliefs all at once. . . . But he feels called upon to justify, explain, demonstrate his attitude, and an element *b* enters in, which in one way or another saves the letter of his beliefs while altering them in substance.

800. The principal element in the situation, the element *a*, is evidently the one to which the human being is most strongly attached and which he exerts himself to justify. That element therefore is the more important to us in our quest for the social equilibrium.

801. But the element *b*, though secondary, also has its effect upon the equilibrium. Sometimes the effect may be so insignificant as to be accounted equivalent to zero—as when the perfection of the number 6 is ascribed to its being the sum of its aliquots (1, 2, 3). But the effect may also be very considerable, as when the Inquisition burned people guilty of some slip in their theological calculations.

802. We have said that the element *b* is made up, in variable proportions, of sentiments and logical inferences. It is well to remark at once that in social matters its persuasive force depends as a rule chiefly on sentiments, the logic being accepted principally because it chances to harmonize with such sentiments. In the logico-experimental sciences, in proportion as they are brought to greater and greater perfection, the part played by sentiment tends to decrease towards zero, and the persuasive force lies altogether in the logic and in the facts. When it reaches that extreme the element *b* evidently changes its character, and we shall designate it by *B*. At another extreme there are cases in which the logical inference is not clearly manifested, as in what jurists call "latent principles in law." Psychologists explain such phenomena as effects of the subconscious, or in some other way. We do not choose to go quite so far back

here; we stop at the fact, leaving the explanation of it to others. All
concrete theories fall between those extremes, approaching the one
or the other to a greater or lesser extent.

. . . . .

863. *Example.* Christians have the custom of baptism. If one knew
the Christian procedure only one would not know whether and
how it could be analyzed. Moreover, we have an explanation of it:
We are told that the rite of baptism is celebrated in order to remove original sin. That still is not enough. If we had no other facts
of the same class to go by, we should find it difficult to isolate the
elements in the complex phenomenon of baptism. But we do have
other facts of that type. The pagans too had lustral water, and
they used it for purposes of purification. If we stopped at that, we
might associate the use of water with the fact of purification. But
other cases of baptism show that the use of water is not a constant
element. Blood may be used for purification, and other substances
as well. Nor is that all; there are numbers of rites that effect the
same result. In cases where taboos have been violated, certain rites
remove the pollution that a person has incurred in one set of circumstances or another. So the circle of similar facts widens, and in
the great variety of devices and in the many explanations that are
given for their use the thing which remains constant is the feeling,
the sentiment, that the integrity of an individual which has been
altered by certain causes, real or imaginary, can be restored by
certain rites. The given case, therefore, is made up of that constant
element, *a*, and a variable element, *b*, the latter comprising the means
that are used for restoring the individual's integrity and the reasonings by which the efficacy of the means is presumably explained. The
human being has a vague feeling that water somehow cleanses moral
as well as material pollutions. However, he does not, as a rule, justify
his conduct in that manner. The explanation would be far too simple.
So he goes looking for something more complicated, more preten-
tious, and readily finds what he is looking for.

864. The nucleus *a*, now that we have found it, is seen to be
made up of a number of elements: first of all an instinct for combinations; people want "to do something about it"—they want to
combine certain things with certain acts. It is a curious fact, also,
that the ties so imagined persist in time. It would be easy enough to
try some new combination every day. Instead there is one combination, fantastic though it be, that tends to prevail and sometimes does

prevail over all competitors. Discernible, finally, is an instinct which inclines people to believe that certain combinations are suited to attaining certain objectives.

. . . . .

868. Before going any farther it might perhaps be advisable to give word-names to the things we have been calling a, b, and c. To designate them by mere letters of the alphabet in a measure embarrasses our discussion and makes it harder to follow. For that reason, and for no other, suppose we call the things a, *residues,* the things b, *derivations,* and the things c, *derivatives.* But we must always and at all times remember that nothing, absolutely nothing, is to be inferred from the proper meanings of those words or their etymologies, that they mean respectively the things a, b, and c and nothing else.

. . . . .

875. The residues a must not be confused with the sentiments or instincts to which they correspond. The residues are the manifestations of sentiments and instincts just as the rising of the mercury in a thermometer is a manifestation of the rise in temperature. Only elliptically and for the sake of brevity do we say that residues, along with appetites, interests, etc., are the main factors in determining the social equilibrium, just as we say that water boils at 100° Centigrade. The completed statements would be: "The sentiments or instincts that correspond to residues, along with those corresponding to appetites, interests, etc., are the main factors in determining the social equilibrium." "Water boils when its calorific state attains the temperature of 100° as registered by a Centigrade thermometer."

2

The Residues

888. *Classification of residues.* Suppose we begin by classifying residues. Present also, of course, in social phenomena, in addition to the sentiments manifested by residues, are appetites, inclinations, and so on. Here we are dealing strictly with the element that corresponds to residues. In that element many, sometimes indeed a great many, simple residues figure, just as rocks contain many simple elements that can be isolated by chemical analysis. In the concrete, one residue may prevail over others in given phenomena, so that they may be taken roughly as representing that residue. The present classification is made from the objective standpoint; but we shall be called upon, here and there, to add some few subjective considerations.

CLASS I: INSTINCT FOR COMBINATIONS

I-α. Generic combinations

I-β. Combinations of similars or opposites

    I-β1. Generic likeness or oppositeness

    I-β2. Unusual things and exceptional occurrences

    I-β3. Objects and occurrences inspiring awe or terror

    I-β4. Felicitous state associated with good things; infelicitous state, with bad

    I-β5. Assimilation: physical consumption of substances to get effects of associable, and more rarely of opposite, character

I-γ. Mysterious workings of certain things; mysterious effects of certain acts

    I-γ1. Mysterious operations in general

    I-γ2. Mysterious linkings of names and things

I-δ. Need for combining residues
I-ε. Need for logical developments
I-ζ. Faith in the efficacy of combinations

CLASS II: GROUP-PERSISTENCES (PERSISTENCE OF AGGREGATES)

II-α. Persistence of relations between a person and other persons
and places
    II-α1. Relationships of family and kindred groups
    II-α2. Relations with places
    II-α3. Relationships of social class
II-β. Persistence of relations between the living and the dead
II-γ. Persistence of relations between a dead person and the things
that belonged to him in life
II-δ. Persistence of abstractions
II-ε. Persistence of uniformities
II-ζ. Sentiments transformed into objective realities
II-η. Personifications
II-θ. Need of new abstractions

CLASS III: NEED OF EXPRESSING SENTIMENTS BY EXTERNAL ACTS
(ACTIVITY, SELF-EXPRESSION)

III-α. Need of "doing something" expressing itself in combinations
III-β. Religious ecstasies

CLASS IV: RESIDUES CONNECTED WITH SOCIALITY

IV-α. Particular societies
IV-β. Need of uniformity
    IV-β1. Voluntary conformity on the part of the individual
    IV-β2. Uniformity enforced upon others
    IV-β3. Neophobia
IV-γ. Pity and cruelty
    IV-γ1. Self-pity extended to others
    IV-γ2. Instinctive repugnance to suffering
    IV-γ3. Reasoned repugnance to useless sufferings
IV-δ. Self-sacrifice for the good of others
    IV-δ1. Risking one's life
    IV-δ2. Sharing one's property with others
IV-ε. Sentiments of social ranking; hierarchy
    IV-ε1. Sentiments of superiors

IV-ε2. Sentiments of inferiors
IV-ε3. Need of group approbation
IV-ζ. Asceticism

CLASS V: INTEGRITY OF THE INDIVIDUAL
AND HIS APPURTENANCES

V-α. Sentiments of resistance to alterations in the social equilibrium
V-β. Sentiments of equality in inferiors
V-γ. Restoration of integrity by acts pertaining to the individual whose integrity has been impaired
  V-γ1. Real subjects
  V-γ2. Imaginary or abstract subjects
V-δ. Restoration of integrity by acts pertaining to the offender (vengeance, "getting even")
  V-δ1. Real offender
  V-δ2. Imaginary or abstract offender

CLASS VI: THE SEX RESIDUE

889. Class I. *Instinct for combinations.* This class embraces the residues corresponding to the instinct for combinations, which is intensely powerful in the human species and has probably been, as it still remains, one of the important factors in civilization. Figuring as a residue in vast numbers of phenomena is an inclination to combine certain things with certain other things. The scientist in his laboratory makes combinations according to certain norms, certain purposes, certain hypotheses, for the most part rational (at times he combines at random). His activity is primarily logical. The ignorant person makes combinations in view of analogies that are mostly fantastic, absurd, childish (and often also by chance). In any event they are in large part non-logical acts. There is an instinct that prompts to combinations in general, for reasons which are fleeting, momentary, undetectable. It deserves a separate classification as our genus I-α. Similar things often, less often opposites, are combined. That gives us a genus I-β. If the similarities or contrasts are generic, we get a species I-β1. Unusual things are often combined with important occurrences (I-β2); or things and happenings alike impressive are brought together (I-β3). A felicitous state attracts good or praiseworthy things, and vice versa (I-β4), whereas an infelicitous contingency attracts bad, unpleasant, horrible things, and vice versa.

In a genus I-γ we place combinations of things and acts that have something mysterious about them, and that genus falls into two species: mysterious operations in general (I-γ1), and mysterious linkings of names with things (I-γ2). The human being feels a need for combining various residues (I-δ). Then again, we note a need that is the more keenly felt the higher the degree of civilization in a people: a need for cloaking acts that are in themselves non-logical with a logical veneer, for devising theories that may be alto gether imaginary so only they be logical. We make a special genus for that: I-ϵ. Finally we have to provide for the belief in the efficacy of combinations (I-ζ). Taking Class I as a whole, one notes: (1) a propensity for combinations; (2) a search for the combinations that are deemed best; (3) a propensity to believe that they actually do what is expected of them.

890. There are, moreover, passive and active aspects to combinations. On the passive side the human being is subject to them; on the active side he interprets, controls, or produces them. The propensity, too, is a vague generic sentiment that operates passively and actively. It may be seen in vigorous action in games of chance among all peoples. There the quest for the best possible combinations is conspicuous and eager. As for the propensity to believe in the efficacy of combinations, it also has a passive and an active aspect. On the passive side, a person may believe that A is necessarily conjoined with B so that if A occurs, B must ensue. On the active side, the idea is that if one can manage to produce A, one can get B as a consequence.

891. In the concrete case residues from other classes also figure, notably residues from Class II. Were it not for the persistence of certain relations, the combinations in Class I would be ephemeral insubstantial things. One might compare the situation to a building. The instinct for combinations, the quest for the best possible one, the faith in its efficacy, provide the materials. Persistence of associations gives stability to the strutcure; it is the cement that holds it together. Then faith in the efficacy of combinations again interposes to incline people to use the building. In many phenomena, especially among civilized peoples, one notes mixtures: logical actions, scientific inferences, non-logical actions, effects of sentiment. Here we are segregating by analysis things that occur in a compound form in concrete reality.

· · · · ·

910. I-β: *Combinations of similars or opposites.* Similarity or contrast in things, no matter whether real or imaginary, is a potent cause of combinations. The reason is at once apparent if one but consider the associations of ideas that such things provoke. Nonlogical reasonings are often reasonings by association of ideas.

911. It is important to note that if A and B are similar things, and C and D their opposites, the phenomenon opposite to the combination A + B is not the combination C + D, but the absence of any combination. The opposite of belief in God is not belief in the Devil, but absence of belief in either. The state of mind of the person who is continually dwelling on matters of sex has its opposite in the state of mind, not of the person who is continually alluding to sex with horror, but of the person no more concerned with it than with any other bodily function.

. . . . .

932. I-β4: *Felicitous state associated with good things; infelicitous state, with bad.* When a given state A is considered a happy one, there is an inclination to associate anything that is deemed good with it. When a state B is considered bad, the tendency is to associate all bad things with it. This residue often goes in company with another residue from Class II (group-persistences). So we get a nucleus, with many notions of good or evil things clustering about it, and so, by a process of abstraction, the way is opened for a personification of the whole nebulous complex whereby it becomes an entity by itself, first existing subjectively in the minds of people, but eventually . . . acquiring an objective existence.

933. For a long time in Europe everything good was placed under the aegis of the "wisdom of the forefathers." Nowadays everything good is credited to "progress." To have a "modern sense" of this or that is to have sound and solid sense. In the old days a man was praised for his "time-honoured virtues." Now he is praised for being a "modern man," or—to use, as some do, a neologism—for having an "up-to-date" outlook on things. It was once to one's credit to act "like a Christian"; today it is praiseworthy to act "like a human being," or better, "in a spirit of broad humanity"—when, for instance, one is defending a thief or a murderer. To succour one's neighbour was formerly a "charitable act"; today it is an "act of humanity." . . .

934. The adversaries of an institution hold it responsible for all the bad that happens. Its friends credit it with all the good. "It is

raining—what a crooked administration!" So says the Opposition. "The weather is fine—what a blessed government!" So the Majority. What denunciations were hurled at the governments of the past in Italy on the matter of taxes, though they were light indeed as compared with taxes that are cheerfully tolerated today! The old Tuscan "liberals" inveighed against the Grand Duke for permitting "the immoral lottery"—see what the poet Giusti wrote on the subject in his ironical "Defence of the Lottery." But stepping into power themselves, they found it altogether natural and moral that an Italian government should run lotteries too.

.   .   .   .   .

966. I-δ: *Hunger for combining residues.* The human being often feels prompted to combine certain residues that are present in his mind. That is a manifestation of a synthetic tendency which is indispensable to practical life. Disjoining residues by analysis is a scientific process of which few people are capable. Ask some individual who is not familiar with scientific method (or even, at a venture, someone who is, or ought to be) to solve the problem as to whether $A = B$. It will be found that almost irresistibly he will be inclined to consider at the same time, and without the slightest effort to keep them separate, other questions, such as: "Is it a good idea that A should be equal to B? Is it better to believe that $A = B$? Does the identification of A and B meet with the approval of certain people? Or do they disapprove?" And so on and on. Take the question, "Will the man who follows the precepts of morality achieve material prosperity?" It is, virtually, impossible for many people to consider such a question by itself.

967. The human being is loath to dissever faith from experience; he wants a completed whole free from discordant notes. For long centuries Christians believed that their Scriptures contained nothing at variance with historical or scientific experience. Some of them have now abandoned that opinion as regards the natural sciences, but cling to it as regards history. Others are willing to drop the Bible as science and history, but insist on keeping at least its morality. Still others will have a much-desired accord, if not literally, at least allegorically, by dint of ingenious interpretations. The Moslems are convinced that all mankind can know is contained in the Koran. The authority of Homer was sovereign for the ancient Greeks. For certain Socialists the authority of Marx is, or at least was, just as supreme. No end of felicitous sentiments are harmonized in a

melodious whole in the Holy Progress and the Holy Democracy of modern peoples.

968. The ancient Epicureans absolutely divorced the residues associated with their gods from other sorts of residues. But that case stands by itself, or is at least very rare. In general, many varieties of residues are blended in concepts of divinity. A similar process of concentration also takes place among the various divinities. That is one of the main forces at work in the development from polytheism to monotheism.

969. The impulse to combine residues plays a not inconsiderable rôle in the use people make of certain words of vague indeterminate meanings but which are supposed to correspond to real things. The term "good," and the kindred term "well-being," are quite generally taken as standing for real things. "Good," at bottom, is something pleasing to the sense of taste. Then the sense circle widens and "good" is anything pleasing to the taste and promotive of physical health, and from that, anything promotive of physical health alone. Then the sense-circle widens again to embrace moral sensations, and they come to dominate in what is considered "good," and in "well-being." In the end, among philosophers and moralists especially, moral sensations are the only ones considered at all. In other words, the terms gradually come to designate a sum of residues towards which the person who uses them chances to feel sentiments of attraction and not of revulsion.

970. In "intellectuals" the impulse to combine residues goes farther still. They make one general blend of "well-being," "the true," "the beautiful," "the good," and some of them add "altruism," "solidarity," "the human," or better yet, the "broadly human," thus forming a simple complex gratifying as a whole to their sentimentality. Then that complex (or any other like it) which rests merely on the need for combinations may, eventually, acquire in virtue of residues of group-persistence (Class II) an independent existence, and in certain cases even be personified [for example, Progress, Democracy, Reason].

971. Far from negligible among the differences obtaining between a scientific research and a piece of literature is the fact that the former separates residues while the latter combines them. Literature satisfies the human hunger for combining residues and that need is left unsatisfied by science. As for the demand for logic . . . one

might guess that it should be better satisfied by science than by literature; and so it may be with some few individuals. But not so for the majority of men. Most people are entirely satisfied with the pseudo-logic of literary compositions. Literature is much better suited to their understanding and their tastes than the exact, rigorous thinking of the experimental method. A scientific work may therefore convince the few specialists who understand the subject with which it deals; but literature is always better able to influence mankind in the mass. . . .

972. I-ε: *Hunger for logical developments.* The demand for logic is satisfied by pseudo-logic as well as by rigorous logic. At bottom what people want is to think—it matters little whether the thinking be sound or fallacious. We need only reflect on the tangle-wood of fantastic discussion that has flourished and still flourishes around such incomprehensible subjects as come up in the various systems of theology and metaphysics—wild speculations as to the Creation, the purposes for which human life was ordained, and such things—to gain some conception of the imperiousness of the need that is satisfied by such lucubrations.

973. Those who proclaim "the bankruptcy of Science" are right in the sense that science cannot satisfy the insatiable need of pseudo-logical developments that the human being feels. Science can merely relate one fact to another. There is always, therefore, a fact at which it comes to a halt. The human imagination refuses to stop there. It insists on going on, insists on drawing inferences even from the ultimate fact, on knowing its "cause," and if it cannot find a real cause it invents an imaginary one.

974. We should not forget that if this insistence on having causes at all costs, be they real or imaginary, has been responsible for many imaginary causes, it has also led to the discovery of real ones. As regards residues, experimental science, theology, metaphysics, fatuous speculations as to the origins and the purposes of things, have a common point of departure: a resolve, namely, not to stop with the last known cause of the known fact, but to go beyond it, argue from it, find or imagine something beyond that limit. Savage peoples have no use for the metaphysical speculations of civilized countries, but they are also strangers to civilized scientific activity; and if one were to assert that but for theology and metaphysics experimental science would not even exist, one could not be easily confuted.

Those three kinds of activity are probably manifestations of one same psychic state, on the extinction of which they would vanish simultaneously.

975. This residue explains the need people feel for covering their non-logical conduct with a varnish of logic—a point we have already stressed time and again and at length. It also accounts for that element in social phenomena which we have designated as *b* and which constitutes the whole subject of derivations. The usual purpose of a derivation, in fact, is to satisfy with pseudo-logic the need of logic, of thinking, that the human being feels.

976. I-ζ: *Faith in the efficacy of combinations.* As we have already noted (§890), one may believe that A is necessarily conjoined with B. That belief may be based on experience, on the fact, that is, that A has always been observed in conjunction with B. From such a fact, however, logico-experimental science infers merely that it is more or less probable that A will always appear in conjunction with B. To ascribe an attribute of "necessity" to the proposition, one has to add to it a something that is non-experimental—an act of faith.

977. That much being granted, if imagination were equivalent to demonstration, the scientist working in his laboratory would note the combinations AB without preconception. But that is not the case. In prosecuting his researches, imagining, inventing, he allows himself to be guided by guesses, assumptions, preconceptions—perhaps even prejudices. That does no harm in the case of the scientist. Experience will be there to rectify any error that may develop from the sentiments he feels.

978. For the person who is not grounded in the logico-experimental method, rôles are inverted. Sentiments now play the leading part. Such a person is chiefly moved by faith in the efficacy of combinations. Oftentimes he is indifferent to experimental verifications. Often again, if he does give them a thought he rests content with utterly insufficient, sometimes even ridiculous, proofs.

979. Such conceptions reign sovereign in the minds of the majority of men, and that is why the mind of the scientist sometimes succumbs to them. That will happen the more readily, the more closely, in the pursuit of his calling, the scientist keeps in touch with the population at large and to the same extent the less aware will he be that his sentimental results are in conflict with experience. That is why the student of the social sciences finds it more difficult to adhere

to the logico-experimental method than, for instance, the chemist or the physicist.

980. But let us ignore the logico-experimental sciences for the present, and look at things from the standpoint of sentiments and residues. If the combination AB is a fact not of the laboratory, but of ordinary life, it will in the long run engender in the minds of people a sentiment linking A indissolubly with B, and such a sentiment is virtually indistinguishable from a sentiment originating outside experience or pseudo-experimentally.

981. If there is a cock in the hen-coop, the eggs will produce chicks. When a cock crows at midnight, someone dies in the house. For the person reasoning on sentiment, those two propositions are equally certain and, for that matter, equally experimental; and the sentiment that dictates them derives in the one case as in the other from direct experience and from indirect experiences reported by other persons. If one objects that a rooster has been known to crow at midnight without anybody's dying, there is the answer that an egg from a hen living with a rooster often fails to produce a chick. The scientist distinguishes the two phenomena not only by direct experience, but also by the check of likeness—(assimilation). The plain man is not equal to that; and even when he declares the belief about the cock crowing at midnight an absurd superstition, he can offer no better reasons that he could when he held it to be an undebatable truth.

982. Speaking in general, the ignorant man is guided by faith in the efficacy of combinations, a faith which is kept alive by the fact that many combinations are really effective, but which none the less arises spontaneously within him, as may be seen in the child that amuses itself by trying the strangest combinations. The ignorant person distinguishes little if at all between effective and ineffective combinations. He bets on lottery numbers according to his dreams just as confidently as he goes to the railroad station at the time designated in the time-table. He thinks it quite as natural to consult the faith-curer or the quack as to consult the most expert physician. . . .

983. As experimental science progresses, people try to give an experimental gloss to the products of their sentiments and assert that their faith in combinations derives from experience. But one need only examine the facts a little closely to see the fatuousness of such explanations.

984. If superstition has on the whole fallen off in the masses in our day, the fact is due not so much directly to the influence of the logico-experimental sciences as indirectly to the prestige of scientists —they meantime having introduced quite a number of new superstitions of their own. And it is partly due to the enormous development of industrial life, which is to a large extent an experimental life and has had the effect of disputing—in no very explicit way, to be sure—the dominion of sentiment.

985. The belief that A must necessarily be linked with B is strengthened and becomes stable in virtue of residues of group-persistence. For the very reason that it is rooted in sentiments it takes over from them the vagueness which is their distinguishing trait; and A and B are oftentimes not definite things, definite acts, but classes of things or acts, usually corresponding to our I-β and I-γ varieties (similars or opposites, mysteries). Hence a thing A is linked to anything B provided it be a similar or an opposite, or exceptional, terrible, propitious, and so on. A comet presages the death of some important person, but who the person is nobody very definitely knows.

986. Whatever the origin of the belief that A is linked to B, whether it be experimental, pseudo-experimental, sentimental, fantastic, or of some other character, once it exists and has been consolidated, stabilized, by the residues of group-persistence, it exerts a powerful influence upon sentiments and conduct, and that in two directions, the one passive, the other active.

987. On the passive side, given one element of the combination AB, the individual is uneasy if the whole combination does not materialize. So, B being posterior to A, on observing A he looks for B (comets, and events announced by them—presages in general). B being given, there is the conviction that it must have been preceded by A, and the past is ransacked until a corresponding A is found (events that were supposed to have foretold the rise of Roman Emperors to the throne). If A and B both lie in the past, they are brought together even if they have nothing whatever to do with each other (presages recorded by historians, when they are not inventions pure and simple).

988. Oftentimes B is left undefined or is defined only to the extent of belonging to a certain class. Something has to happen—exactly what no one really knows. Under pressure of group-persistences the

combination *AB* has acquired a personality of its own, independent, within certain limits, of *B*.

989. On the active side there is a feeling that if one can get *A*, one can get *B*. In that way the passive science of divination becomes the active science of sorcery. The Romans already had introduced an active element into divination through their rules for accepting or rejecting presages. Not all combinations lend themselves to such transformation. In the first place, combinations in which *A* does not lie within human powers—thunder, for instance, or the appearance of a comet—are of course barred. But there are cases even when *A* does lie within human powers where there is no belief that *B* can be obtained by use of *A*. A superhuman being is born of a virgin, but no one believes that a virgin will always yield such a child. It took thirty-six hours or more to engender Hercules, but no one imagines that by exerting onself to that same extent one will as a matter of course beget a son of Herculean stature. There are cases, then, where there is a mixture of the active and the passive—words of good omen, for instance. If they are heard accidentally, they presage good fortune. It is also a good idea to utter them deliberately, to facilitate the advent of good fortune. Similarly, but vice versa, for words of evil omen.

. . . . .

991. Class II: *Group-persistences* (Persistence of aggregates). Certain combinations constitute a group of elements closely united as in one body, so that the compound ends by acquiring a personality such as other real entities have. Such combinations may often be recognized by the fact of their having names of their own, distinct from the mere enumeration of their component elements. The presence of such a name in its turn gives greater consistency to the concept of the group as a personality, by virtue of a residue which assumes that a name always has a thing corresponding to it. The sentiments associated with the group may remain virtually constant, but they may also vary in intensity and in diffusion. Such variation must be kept distinct from that other and much greater variability which affects the forms in which the sentiments express themselves —from variability in derivations, in other words. There is, briefly, first, a nucleus, which has a personality of its own but which may vary, much as a chick varies in becoming a hen, or a caterpillar in becoming a butterfly; and then, second, there are the manifestations under forms of derivations of that nucleus, and they would corre-

spond to the capriciously varying conduct of the chick or the caterpillar.

992. After the group has been constituted, an instinct very often comes into play that tends with varying energy to prevent the things so combined from being disjoined, and which, if disintegration cannot be avoided, strives to dissemble it by preserving the outer physiognomy of the aggregate. This instinct may be compared roughly to mechanical inertia: it tends to resist the movement imparted by other instincts. To that fact the tremendous social importance of Class II residues is to be ascribed.

993. Combinations that disintegrate as soon as they are formed do not constitute groups of subsisting individuality. But if they do persist, they end by acquiring that trait. Not by abstraction only do they take on a sort of individuality, any more than by abstraction only do we recognize groups of sensations by such names as "hunger," "wrath," or "love," or a number of sheep by the name of "flock." The point must be clearly grasped. There is nothing corresponding to the noun "flock," in the sense that the flock may be separated from the sheep which constitute it. At the same time the flock is not a mere equivalent to the sum of the sheep. The sheep, by the very fact that they are members of the flock, acquire characteristics which they would not have apart from it. A male and a female thrown together at an age for reproduction are something different from the same male and female taken by themselves. Yet that does not mean that there is an entity X distinct from male and female which represents the male and the female coupled.

994. To these considerations must be added another, to which frequent reference has already been made in these pages, namely, that though the abstraction corresponding to the group may not have an objective existence, it may have a subjective existence, and that fact is most important in its bearing on the social equilibrium. An example will make that clear. Let us imagine that certain people have taken a river for their god. The fact may be explained in a great variety of ways: a. It may be said that by a process of abstraction the people in question have distinguished from the concrete river an ideal river that they regard as "a force of nature" and worship as such. b. It may be said that they have ascribed human attributes to the river, assuming that it has a soul, just as a man is assumed to have a soul, and that that soul has been deified. c. It may be said that the river has given rise within the people in question

to a variety of sensations to an extent at least not clearly defined, but very potent. These sensations persist, and their sum, their combination, their aggregate, constitutes, for the subject and for those people, a thing to which they have given a name, just as people give names to all other subjective things deemed worthy of their notice. This entity together with its name is attracted by other similar entities and may take its place in the pantheon of the people, just as it may take its place near the flag in the patriotic aggregate (the German Rhine), or a more modest place in the baggage-train of the poets. No one of these three manners of approach is to be barred; but the third explains a number of facts that are not accounted for by the other two, and which sometimes even stand in conflict with them. The residue underlying the third hypothesis is therefore much more generally used than the other two residues.

995. We came upon cases of this kind on a previous occasion in our discussion of the gods of ancient Rome; and we saw that they corresponded to certain associations of acts and ideas. We now carry the analysis a step further, and see in those cases residues of Class I which have become permanent under pressure of residues of Class II. A cult of that type is a sort of fetishism where the fetish is not a thing, but an act. If we tried to explain it by hypotheses *a* or *b*, we should never succeed in understanding how the Roman, whose mind was undoubtedly more practical, less subtle, less ingenious than the Greek mind, could have come out with so many abstractions, seen everywhere about him so many "forces of nature" (probably not even having the remotest notion corresponding to that term!), and so shown himself more idealistic than the Greek. It would seem, indeed, that the opposite should be the case. On the hypothesis *c*, the facts are very readily explainable. Class II residues were much stronger among the Romans than among the Greeks. Hence it ought to follow—and it actually has followed—that a larger number of aggregates would acquire independent individuality, and it is such aggregates, precisely, that have been passed off as "personifications of forces of nature" by rationalizing historians far surpassing in subtlety of mind the rough and rude people among whom the associations in question originated.

996. We find inscriptions to the goddess Annona (the year's crop). It seems hard to believe that by a process of abstraction the Romans should have personified the victualling of Rome, and then have proceeded to exalt the personification to divine rank. One

readily sees, however, how strong and deep-seated the sensations associated with the maintenance of a food-supply at once so important and so difficult must have been. They came to constitute a group, which by the fact of permanency acquired an individuality of its own—became a *thing*. That thing, eventually, under its name, Annona, took its place with many other things of the same kind in the Roman pantheon.

. . . . .

1015. II-α: *Persistence of relations between a person and other persons and places.* This variety falls into three subvarieties presenting similar and closely related characteristics, so that the residues readily blend and they also compensate one for the other. These residues are common to men and animals. It is said that certain animals have a sense of "property," which is just a way of saying that they have a permanent sentiment attaching them to places and things. Also persistent in them is a sentiment attaching them to people and to other animals. The dog knows not only his master, but other individuals and animals about the house. A dog kennelled in a garden will not harm the cats and the poultry that belong there. Once outside the gate he chases all the cats and hens he sees; and he will attack a strange cat that enters his garden. In a case I have in mind, a number of cocks hatched in the same brood and kept together did not fight. One of them was taken away and kept apart for six days. It was taken for granted that he could be put back with the others as a matter of course, but he was immediately attacked and killed. The same thing happened with two male cats that were born together and lived together peacefully. They were separated for a short time. When they were again brought together they went at each other furiously. The human sentiments of family, so called, of property, patriotism, love for the mother-tongue, for the ancestral religion, for friends, and so on, are of just that character, except that the human being dresses his sentiments up with derivations and logical explanations that sometimes conceal the residue.

. . . . .

1052. II-β: *Persistence of relations between the living and the dead.* The sum of relations between an individual and other individuals persists, by abstraction, in the absence of that individual or after his death. That explains residues which figure in vast numbers of phenomena. They are in some respects similar to II-α residues, and that explains why they are found combined with them in many

many cases, such as family, caste, patriotism, religion, and so on. In combination with IV-δ2 residues, which prompt sharing of possessions with the objects of one's love or goodwill, they appear in such complex phenomena as honouring or worshipping the dead, or banquets and sacrifices connected with funerals or commemorations.

1053. Those who will have logical explanations for all human beliefs imagine that such phenomena presuppose belief in the immortality of the soul, for without such a postulate they would not be logical. To refute that notion, one need merely observe, ignoring countless other proofs, that among the people right about us, materialists are not less punctilious than others in honouring their dead, in spite of their philosophy; and that in London and Paris, to say nothing of other cities, there are cemeteries for dogs where such pets are buried by people who certainly do not credit the dog with an immortal soul.

1054. Ghosts, apparitions of the dead, which have at all times been taken seriously more or less everywhere, are nothing but tangible forms given to residues of persisting relations between the living and the dead, which by analogy also figure to some extent in apparitions of divinities, angels, devils, fairies, and other personified entities of the kind. . . .

1055. It is apparent, on close scrutiny, that the concept of the survival of the dead is at bottom merely the extension of another notion which is very powerful in the human being, the notion that the individuality of a person is a unit over the course of the years. In reality both the physical and the psychic elements in the human being change. Neither materially nor morally is an aged man identical with the child he was. And yet we feel that in him there is something which endures the same. Overstepping the experimental field, people call it a "soul," without being able to explain very clearly what becomes of such a soul in lunacy, for example, or in "second childhood," or just when, between the time when the human egg is fertilized and the first cry of the new-born babe, such a soul finds its way into the body. Such matters need not concern us here, since they transcend the confines of the experimental field within which we have chosen to remain. Our point is merely to show that one same residue is present in the belief in the unity of the living individuality and in the belief in survival after death.

· · · · ·

1065. II-δ: *Persistence of abstractions.* After an agglomerate of relations has grown up, either in the manner described in §991 or in some other, a corresponding abstraction appears that may persist in time; and then a new subjective entity comes into being.

1066. Such residues underlie theologies and systems of metaphysics, which might properly be defined as cumuli of derivations from such residues. Hence the great importance of theologies and metaphysical systems—not the importance they are supposed to have when considered as logical sciences, but as expressing residues that correspond to powerful social forces.

1067. From that standpoint past and present alike show remarkable uniformity. There is, however, a difference in the matter of personification of abstractions, which among our Western people was far more characteristic of the past than it is of more recent times. Let us glance at one or two abstractions that are so important as to deserve classification by themselves.

1068. II-ε: *Persistence of uniformities.* An important instance of the persistence of abstractions is the common procedure of generalizing a particular uniformity or even a single, isolated fact. A fact is observed. It is stated in abstract language. The abstraction persists and becomes a general rule. The thing is a matter of everyday occurrence. We may even go so far as to say that that is the characteristic manner of reasoning of people not trained to scientific thinking and even of many who are. Very few people indeed state particular facts under particular forms, and are able to distinguish that form of expression from the other which states a general rule, and furthermore to distinguish the rule that is an instrument of research and subject to experimental verification from the rule that is assumed to be above such verification. Going to extremes in the direction of abstractions superior to experience, we get metaphysical principles, "natural" principles, "necessary" relationships, and the like.

1069. II-ζ: *Sentiments transformed into objective realities.* Such residues are exceedingly numerous, so much so that they are rarely absent from any discussion that is not conducted with strictest scientific exactitude. They underlie all subjective proofs derived from sentiments, and they exert a powerful influence upon the considerations that inspire the production and acceptance of theories. The introspection of the metaphysicist, the "inner experience" of the Christian, and other similar manners of thinking, all involve transformations of sentiments into objective realities.

1070. II-η: *Personifications.* The lowest degree of personification lies in the naming of an abstraction, a uniformity, or a sentiment, and so transforming them into objective individualities. Thence, step by step, we mount to the highest degree, where the personification is complete and we get anthropomorphism. Bringing in the sex residue we get male and female principles, or divinities in every respect similar to men and women. Places and things may also be personified, without there being on that account any deification. Such personifications arise spontaneously in the mind independently of any process of reasoning.

1071. Language is a very effective instrument for lending continuity to such groups and for personifying them; and the mere bestowal of a name on a sum of abstractions is often sufficient to transform it into an objective individuality. Conversely, every name is supposed to have some such reality corresponding to it. Language also may play a part in endowing the abstractions with sex, but the sex residue is itself sufficient to account for that development. Language thereupon comes in to determine what the sex shall be.

. . . . .

1089. Class III: *Need of expressing sentiments by external acts.* Powerful sentiments are for the most part accompanied by certain acts that may have no direct relation to the sentiments but do satisfy a need for action. Something similar is observable in animals. A cat moves its jaws at sight of a bird; the dog twists and turns and wags its tail at sight of its master; the parrot flaps its wings.

1090. Says Lyall further: "The present writer knew a Hindu officer of great shrewdness and very fair education who devoted several hours daily to the elaborate worship of five round pebbles which he had appointed to be his symbol of Omnipotence. Although his general belief was in one all-pervading Divinity, he must have something symbolic to handle and address." Notable in that is not merely the need for the symbol, but the need for "doing something," acting, moving the limbs, fixing the attention on something concrete—escaping, in a word, from a state of passive abstraction. In our day, Flammarion and other scientists hold a meeting at the spring equinox and watch a sunrise.

1091. The acts in which sentiments express themselves reinforce such sentiments and may even arouse them in individuals who were without them. It is a well known psychological fact that if an emotion finds expression in a certain physical attitude, an individual putting himself in that attitude may come to feel the corresponding emotion. The residues of this class, accordingly, stand conjoined with emotions, sentiments, and passions in a complex concatenation of actions and reactions.

. . . . .

1113. Class IV: Residues connected with sociality. This class is made up of residues connected with life in society. Disciplinary residues might also be grouped here, if one agrees that the sentiments corresponding to them are strengthened by living in society. In that direction, it has been observed that with the exception of the cat all domestic animals when at liberty live in groups. On the other hand society is impossible without some sort of discipline, and therefore the social structure and the disciplinary structure necessarily have certain points of contact.

. . . . .

1115. IV-β: Need of uniformity. That need is felt also by animals that live in society. If a hen is painted red and returned to its flock, the other hens at once attack it. The need of uniformity is much more strongly felt among uncivilized than among civilized peoples.

1116. In human societies the uniformity desired may be general throughout a people, but it may also differ according to the various groupings of individuals within the people. We get a picture of the, situation in the crystallization of salt solutions. Around a central nucleus successive stratifications cluster to form a thick crystal. But there is not one crystal only in the solution; there are a number of crystals. In the same way there is not one centre of similarity in a given society, but a number of centres. Sometimes there is conflict between the different "sets," the one trying to extend its own particular uniformity to others. Then again there is no such conflict, each individual resting content with the uniformity of the group to which he belongs and respecting others.

. . . . .

1127. The requirement of uniformity is particularly assertive in matters of logic. From the logical standpoint the maximum of absurdity would seem to be reached in condemning a man to the stake because he does not think as others think on some theological question that is incomprehensible to any rational human being. But that criticism is valid only for the derivation, for the logical reason devised to explain what has been done. The act itself is just the manifestation of a sentiment of hostility to a violation, regarded as particularly flagrant, of a uniformity. Today transgressors of that kind are no longer burned at the stake, because the whole scale of penalties has been lowered; but people who preach birth-control are sent to prison. One is allowed to deny the actual presence of Christ in the Host, but not to believe that if a man is not well enough off to support children, he would do better to keep them from coming into the world and use measures calculated to prevent conception.

. . . . .

1130. IV-β_3: *Neophobia.* This is a sentiment of hostility to innovations that are calculated to disturb uniformities. It is very very powerful among uncivilized or barbarous peoples, and shows a very considerable strength among civilized peoples, being surpassed only by the instinct for combinations (Class I residues).

1131. In Paris in February, 1911, women who appeared on the streets in *jupe-culottes* ("bloomers") were attacked and beaten by mobs. Similar incidents took place in Italy and Spain, and more or less everywhere. Much the same things had happened previously when "picture hats" first came into vogue, and on occasions of other innovations in fashion.

1132. It is interesting that many individuals who suffer from neophobias in some departments of life may look with favour upon anything new in some other direction, say in politics or religion, and for the simple reason that it is new. They are shocked at innovations in tailoring and dressmaking, but fume at the mouth because the Pope does not take kindly to the innovations of the Modernists, and heap abuse on governments that make haste slowly in adopting "social reforms." Fresh proof that contradictory residues can function simultaneously in the mind of one same person! In the case just mentioned the conflict is between the residues of neophobia and the residues of the religion of Progress.

. . . . .

1153. IV-ϵ: *Sentiments of social ranking (hierarchy).* Sentiments of ranking on the part of inferiors as well as superiors are observable in animals. They are very wide-spread in human societies. It would seem indeed that no human society at all complex could survive without them. Relationships of superiority and inferiority are changed in forms, but none the less kept, in societies that ostensibly proclaim equality for all individuals. A sort of temporary feudalism is the rule in such societies, with a progressive descent in rankings from the politicians at the top to the politicians at the bottom. Any-

one doubting this need only try to obtain something, in Italy or
France for instance, without the support of the local "boss," the
Deputy in the parliament, the "powers that be" in art, science, or
public service; or (at the bottom of the ladder) the "fixer." With
sentiments of social ranking we may class the sentiment of deference
the individual feels for the group of which he is a part, or for other
groups, and his desire to have their approval or admiration.

.   .   .   .   .

1160. IV-ϵ3: *Need of group approbation.* This is one of the cases
in which the difference between the sentiment and the manifestation
of it which constitutes the residue comes out most clearly. The need
that the individual feels for being well regarded by his group, for
winning its approval, is a very powerful sentiment. On it human
society may be said to rest. But it works in silence, oftentimes without being expressed. Indeed the person who most desires admiration
—glory—from his group pretends to be indifferent to it. Strange as
it may seem, he may really be indifferent to it, and then again unwittingly allow himself to be guided by the approbation or admiration of others. That is observable in ascetics who are such in good
faith.

1161. The sentiments of sociality manifested by various sorts of
residues are nearly always accompanied by a desire for the approbation of others, or for avoiding their censure. But it is not very usual
for this latter sentiment to express itself in the residue corresponding
to it. Conversely, the residue sometimes hides other residues. A person may say that he is prompted by a desire to win the esteem of
others, whereas to some extent, however slight, he is also prompted
by a desire to do the thing that after all merits such esteem. When
a person does a thing and says, "It is good," or refrains from doing
a thing and says, "It is bad," it is hard to say whether he means, "It
is approved (or disapproved) by the group," or that it accords or
disaccords with his own sentiments. The two considerations function
simultaneously. As a rule the approbation or censure of the group
reinforces a sentiment already present in the individual. There may,
of course, be the perfect hypocrite who is loath to do a thing but
does it to win public esteem. There may be the coward who lets himself be killed in war to escape the stigma of cowardice. But such cases
are not, after all, very frequent. In the commoner case, a person has
a faint impulse to do a thing and does it to win public esteem, or the

naturally brave man is inspired to heroism and gives his life in the thought of glory.

1162. The cases just noted where the individual is not at all, or not entirely, inspired by the sentiment corresponding to the residue that happens to be involved, but entirely or in part by the desire to win the approbation or escape the censure of his group, none the less shows the social importance of the sentiments corresponding to the residues in question. For if the residue is not acting upon the individual directly, it is doing so indirectly through the approbation or censure of the group; and only because that sentiment is influential in the group does the approbation or censure have its force.

. . . . .

1207. Class V: *Integrity of the individual and his appurtenances and possessions.* This class is in a sense the complement of Class IV (sociality). To defend one's own things and strive to increase their quantity are two operations that frequently merge. So defence of integrity and development of personality are two operations that may differ little or even be one and the same. . . .

1208. V-*a*: *Sentiments of resistance to alterations in the social equilibrium.* The equilibrium may be one actually existing, or an ideal equilibrium desired by the individual. But whether real or imaginary, if it is altered, or thought of as altered, the individual suffers, even if he is not directly affected by the alteration, and sometimes, though rarely, even if he gains by it.

. . . . .

1210. If an existing state of social equilibrium is altered, forces tending to re-establish it come into play—that, no more, no less, is what equilibrium means. Such forces are, in chief, sentiments that find their expression in residues of the variety we are here examining. On the passive side, they make us aware of the alteration in the equilibrium. On the active side, they prompt us to remove, repel, counteract, the causes of the alteration, and so develop into sentiments of the V-δ variety. The forces (or sentiments) that come into play when the social equilibrium is disturbed are nearly always perceived by the individual members of that society under some special form. Needless to say, they, as individuals, know nothing about any forces, nothing about any equilibrium. Those are just names which we, as scientists, apply to what is going on. They are conscious of an unpleasant disturbance—it may sometimes be painful, and very painful indeed—of their integrity as it was when the state of equilibrium was still being maintained. Ordinarily such sensations belong to the vague categories known as the "just" or the "unjust." When a person says: "That thing is unjust," what he means is that the thing is offensive to his sentiments as his sentiments stand in the state of social equilibrium to which he is accustomed.

. . . . .

1213. The residue we are here examining prompts a remark of great importance, though it may not appear so at first blush. Take a society in which murder is becoming a frequent occurrence. That society is evidently breaking up. To check the process of dissolution, the sentiment corresponding to our residue does not have to come into play. The immediate interest of the members of the society is enough. In ordinary parlance it will be said that the individual who opposes that state of things is not inspired by any "ideal of justice," but by his instinct of self-preservation, an instinct that he shares with animals and which has nothing to do with any "ideal" of "justice." Now take a very large community where the number of murders is very small. The probability that a given individual will be the victim of a murder is very slight, equal, let us say, to the probability of his succumbing to any number of other perils—of his being bitten by a mad dog, or killed in a railroad accident, things to which the individual pays little attention. The sentiment of direct self-preservation has but slight influence in this case. But another sentiment comes into play and functions vigorously: a sentiment of revulsion against anything disturbing to the social equilibrium as it has existed and is accepted by the individual.

1214. If that sentiment did not exist, every slight incipient alteration in the social equilibrium would meet little or no resistance, and could therefore go on growing with impunity until it came to affect a sufficiently large number of individuals to provoke their resistance from a direct concern to avoid the evil. That is what happens to a certain extent in every society, however highly civilized. But the extent to which it happens is minimized by the interposition of the sentiment of resistance to any alteration in equilibrium, regardless of the number of individuals directly affected. As a consequence the social equilibrium becomes much more stable, and a much more energetic action develops as soon as any alteration sets in.

1215. Examples of such phenomena are exceedingly numerous. One of the most recent was provided by France in 1912. For many

years criminals had been treated with ever increasing indulgence in
the country. The lay school had become a pulpit for Anarchy, and
the social fabric was breaking down in many other respects. The
effects became apparent in cases of "sabotage" in the ship-yards and
on the railways, and finally in the exploits of a gang of Anarchists,
Bonnot, Garnier, and Co. Then some slight reaction occurred. Undoubtedly fear of direct danger on the part of inhabitants of Paris
and the suburbs had something to do with it; but, after all, the
probability of any given citizen's being struck down by such criminals was very very slight. What interposed with greatest effect was
the sentiment of opposition to disturbance of the social equilibrium
as it had been. That feeling, in human society, is somewhat analogous to the instinct in animals that makes them flee at perception of
danger.

1216. It is readily understandable, therefore, that through a combination of this residue of equilibrium with the residues of our Class
II (group-persistences) compound residues of great social importance are built up, corresponding to vigorous and powerful sentiments of the type very vaguely designated by the term "ideal of
justice." From the logico-experimental standpoint to say that an "in-
justice," whether done to one person or to many, involves an equal
offence against "justice," is to say a thing that has no meaning.
There is no such person as "Justice," and one cannot imagine what
"offences" could possibly be offered her. But the wording only is
faulty. At bottom what is expressed is a feeling, vague and instinc-
tive to be sure, that it is a good thing that resistance to disturbances
of the social order should not stand in direct ratio to the number of
individuals affected, but should have a considerable force independent of any such number.

. . . . .

1220. V-β: *Sentiments of equality in inferiors.* This sentiment is
often a defence of integrity on the part of an individual belonging
to a lower class and a means of lifting him to a higher. That takes
place without any awareness, on the part of the individual experiencing the sentiment, of the difference between his real and his
apparent purposes. He talks of the interest of his social class instead
of his own personal interest simply because that is a fashionable
mode of expression.

1221. Striking tendencies arise from the very character of this
sentiment, and at first glance they might seem to be contradictory.

On the one hand there is a tendency to make the largest possible number of persons share in the advantages that the individual asks for himself. On the other, there is a tendency to restrict that number as far as possible. The contradiction disappears the moment we consider that the tendency is to admit to the advantages all whose cooperation helps one towards obtaining them, so that their introduction yields more in profits than it costs; and to exclude all who do not help, or help less effectively, so that their participation costs more than it yields. Similarly, in a war it is a good thing to have as many soldiers as possible for the fighting, and as few as possible for the division of the spoils. Demands for equality almost always conceal demands for privileges.

1222. There is another apparent contradiction. Inferiors wish to be the equals of their superiors, but they will not allow their superiors to be their equals. . . . But the contradiction disappears on reflection that the demand for equality is nothing but a disguised manner of demanding a privilege. The member of one class who demands equality for that class with some other really intends to win it a privilege as compared with the other. If the proposition $A = B$ really means that $A > B$, it is in no way contradictory—in fact, it is the perfection of logic—to go on and say that $B < A$. People agitate for equality to get equality in general, and then go on to make countless numbers of distinctions to deny it in the particular. Equality is to belong to all—but it is granted only to the few.

1223. . . . Among the peoples of our day equality of all human beings is an article of faith; but that does not preclude great differences, in Italy and France, between "union" and "non-union" working-men, between plain citizens and citizens who have "influence" with Deputies, Senators, "grand electors" (local bosses), and the like. Before handing down decisions, judges look well to see with just whom they are dealing. There are gaming-resorts that the police dare not enter, because they would be sure to find law-makers and other important persons there. . . . So in a day gone by it was legal for the nobleman to carry arms, not so for serf or villein.

1224. Such things are known to everybody. That in fact is why no attention is paid to them, why if some Simple Simon ventured to complain of them, people would laugh at him as at someone complaining of the weather. Yet that does not prevent them from believing, in all good faith, that they are enjoying equality. There are hotels in certain places in the United States where a person cannot have his boots polished because it is an offence against Holy Equality for one person to polish another's boots. But the very people who cherish that lofty doctrine of equality are eager to expel the Chinese and Japanese from the United States; are disgusted at the very thought of a Japanese schoolboy sitting at a desk near child of theirs; will not allow a Negro to be accommodated at a hotel that they frequent, or ride in a railway coach which has the honour of transporting them. The thing would seem incredible if it were not true—but there are those among these fierce believers in Holy Equality who hold that Jesus died to redeem all men (and they call them "brethren in Christ"), and who give their mite to missionaries to go out and convert people in Africa and Asia, yet who refuse to worship their God in an American church to which a Negro is admitted.

. . . . .

1226. We are not concerned here with the social utility of such measures. It may be great even if the arguments with which people try to support them are absurd. Then again, it may be nil. Just here we are examining these reasonings merely with reference to the sentiments that inspire them. If the reasonings are patently false but are nevertheless approved and accepted, the fact cannot be due to their logical force but simply to the strength of the sentiments that they hide. That is the fact which it is so important to grasp.

1227. The sentiment that is very inappropriately named equality is fresh, strong, alert, precisely because it is not, in fact, a sentiment of equality and is not related to any abstraction, as a few naïve "intellectuals" still believe; but because it is related to the direct interests of individuals who are bent on escaping certain inequalities not in their favour, and setting up new inequalities that will be in their favour, this latter being their chief concern.

. . . . .

1312. *V-δ: Restoration of integrity by acts pertaining to the offender.* There is a sentiment that impels animals and human beings to hurt those who have hurt them, to return evil for evil. Until that has been done a person experiences a sense of discomfort, as if something were wrong with him. His integrity has been altered, and it does not recover its original state until he has performed certain acts pertaining to his aggressor. Typical are the sentiments underlying vendettas or duels.

1313. *V-δ1: Real offender.* This is by far the most important variety, in fact virtually the only one we need to consider. The offence frequently affects more or less extensive groups even if it is done to one individual member. Relatives of the victim, his dependents, companions, fellow citizens, and even animals—the dog defending its master, for example—may feel the offence as done to them, that their integrity has been altered; and so the need of a restoration of integrity may arise in them and prompt them to react against the offender. Whence, in their many varieties, the obligation of vengeance and the right to blood-money, which are observable among barbarous or semi-civilized peoples. Such residues often blend with the residues of the V-α variety (social equilibrium). Even among civilized peoples of our day, if a citizen of one country is harmed in a foreign country his government often takes the offence as a pretext for exacting indemnity. That is a mere logical act. But many people are led to approve of it by the identical sentiment that in olden times made vengeance a duty. A European is murdered in an uncivilized country. A village where none of the guilty parties are to be found is bombarded and numbers of innocent people are killed. The integrity of the citizens of the civilized country is restored at the expense of the inhabitants of the uncivilized country. The sum of sentiments designated by the term "hatred" may be at least partially classed with this variety. Fear very often lies at the bottom of hatred both in men and in animals. In many cases when the fear goes, hatred turns to contempt. In general terms, hatred arises from a desire to repel an attack on one's integrity. Vigorous conviction is an element in integrity, and that explains the violence of theological hatreds. Hatred wanes when faith wanes, or when the individual no longer considers the faith an essential part of his personality. The artist, the writer, the poet, are led not only by vanity, but also by a profound feeling for their arts, to see an offence to their individual integrity in any contrary expression of opinion, or even in mere silence. Oftentimes any change in the existing state of things is deemed an offence and is repelled by attachment to tradition—neophobia.

     . . . . .

1317. An individual who is barred from a group finds that his integrity has been altered in that simple fact, and the alteration may be felt so keenly as to serve as a very heavy penalty indeed. Even though there is no actual exclusion, the mere declaration that a person's integrity no longer subsists may be equivalent to a penalty inflicted by force.

1318. That explains why in a number of primitive legal systems sentences without sanctions of any kind, and for the execution of which no public authority is designated, are quite the rule. Jurists who are surprised at such things need only reflect that in our own day we still have decisions by "courts of honour" which are of the very same nature. There is no force of public authority to execute such decisions. The mere statement of one may be a penalty much more severe than the day or so in prison inflicted by formal sentence of an ordinary court. There may be indirect sanctions for a sentence that has no direct sanctions, for the integrity of the individual upon whom it bears is altered by it, and in consequence of it he no longer stands on a par with other individuals previously his equals. But such a consequence is in any event accessory. The prime fact is that integrity has been declared altered by certain authorized persons. Caesar, *De bello Gallico*, VI, 13, observed that in Gaul sentences passed by the Druids derived their force from just such indirect consequences. He might have compared that with the *nota censoria* of the Romans or with the *sacer esto* declaration of ancient Roman law. In the concrete case a number of different residues are usually operative. But outstanding in the instances mentioned is a residue whereby the wrongdoer is declared stripped of his integrity. He loses status: he is expelled from the group.

. . . . .

1324. Class VI: *The sex residue.* Mere sexual appetite, though powerfully active in the human race, is no concern of ours here. . . . We are interested in it only in so far as it influences theories, modes of thinking—as a residue. In general terms, the sex residue and the sentiments in which it originates figure in huge numbers of phenomena, but they are often dissembled, especially among modern peoples.

1325. Graeco-Roman antiquity thought of the sexual act as satisfying a bodily need, on a par with eating, drinking, adorning one's person, and the like; and all such things the ancients regarded with indifference, generally condemning abuses, and less frequently excessive refinements, in pleasures. A passage in an oration of Demosthenes against Neaera has remained famous: "We have," says he, "hetairae for our pleasures, concubines for the daily health of the body, wives to give us legitimate children and faithfully to attend to our households." . . . Later on, towards the end of the Roman Empire, and for causes that are still in part obscure, considerations of sex became a tyrannical obsession in the minds of men and assumed religious forms, often asserting themselves as a sort of religious horror. It is a curious fact that among the civilized peoples of our day the sex religion has survived as the last to which the support of the secular arm is still lent. One may blaspheme God and the saints with impunity, one may preach civil war, destruction, expropriation—but one cannot publish obscene books or licentious pictures. . . . Such an inverting of the scale of seriousness in crimes—and an inversion it can only seem to a person not sharing certain religious sentiments—is an essential trait in the punishment of religious heresies and an index of the sway the persecuting instinct exerts over men who are playthings of their prejudices and feelings.

1326. In our Western races three abstinence taboos come down across the ages, and in order of increasing virulence: abstinence from meat, abstinence from wine, abstinence from everything pertaining to sex. Abstinence from meat can be traced as far back as Pythagoras. Surviving from Plutarch are two tracts against the use of meat, De esu animalium (Goodwin, Vol. V, pp. 3–16), to say nothing of a whole treatise on the same subject by Porphyry. The Christians recommended abstinence from meat and enforced it in one form or another. Last in line come the vegetarians of our own day. There was a great deal of talk in ancient times on moderation in the use of wine, but little or none on total abstinence. The early Christians advised a moderate use of wine, or indeed abstinence from it as well as from meat, first as a means of doing penance, but also and more especially as a means of attenuating impulses to carnal sin. There are plenty of prescriptions in such regards by the Church Fathers. However, the Catholic Church has always aimed at a golden mean. Requiring abstinence from meat on certain days, it permitted the use of wine, so showing itself more liberal than many a modern pseudo-scientist. The prohibitionists of our time are re-enacting the feats of the religious fanatics of old. Abstinence from amorous indulgences and from everything even remotely calculated to suggest them is observable, in theory at least, among the early Christians, and in our day, still in theory, it has again given rise to a pathological fanaticism of purity.

1327. Residues in these phenomena are compounds. At least three elements are discernible in them.

1. Least important is a residue of combinations, in view of which members of a sect have some sign or other to distinguish them from the generality of men, from outsiders, from members of other sects. Prohibitions of certain foods are observable among many many peoples. The Bible prohibits the flesh of the hare. No consideration of asceticism or the like can be detected in the prohibition—it is a plain residue of combinations. That residue is often combined with another relating to personal integrity—to pride. The compound serves not only to distinguish, but to glorify. Residues of that sort may very probably have figured in the effort of the Christians to keep themselves distinct from the heathen.

2. The element most important for the first two taboos (meat and wine), and of considerable importance for the third as well (sex), is a residue of asceticism. It manifests its presence in the fact that such taboos are accompanied by abstentions and mortifications that certainly belong to asceticism. That is strikingly apparent in the case of the Christians, less apparent in other abstainers, barely if at all perceptible in still others. The prohibitionists of our day pretend to be interested strictly in public welfare. But it is by no mere chance that they are also as a rule humanitarians, religious zealots, moralists, and champions of sexual purity. Not a few of them, though they may not be aware of it, may not be altogether unaffected by the ascetic residue.

3. Sentiments incidental to asceticism, such as conceit, envy of others who are enjoying what one cannot afford, eagerness for the esteem and admiration of this or that group, and so on.

4. A need for expressing one's faith, in this case an ascetic faith, by external acts (Class III residues, §888).

1328. Religious exaltation sometimes figures in the three taboos. The meat taboo assumes a religious form in India, not so in our Western countries. Scattered examples in connexion with the wine taboo are observable here and there among our contemporaries. With the sex taboo the fact is general all the way along from antiquity down to our own time.

1329. There are actually localities where the meat and wine taboos are more or less scrupulously observed, where, that is, groups of people actually abstain from meat and fermented drinks. For that matter, in such communities or countries the abstinence is at times merely apparent, as is the case in present-day Turkey. But as regards the sex taboo, differences in substance are negligible, there being notable differences only in forms. Prostitution is prohibited in Mohammedan countries, but it has substitutes in concubinage and in even worse practices. It was also prohibited in our parts of the world in days when morals were far from being better than they are at present. The sex taboo is one of the many cases in which sentiments are so powerful as to render substance virtually constant, admitting only of changes in forms. The contrast is so great that one is tempted to adopt the paradox that immorality is greatest there, precisely, where it is most severely condemned by morality and by law. Many indications lead to the belief that that is true of several states in the American Union—though one should not derive a general law from particular instances.

1330. In the religion of sex, as in many other religions, inflexibility in forms gives rise to perversion and hypocrisy; the fable of the forbidden fruit is of all periods of history. In the Middle Ages, and even somewhat later, when religious frenzies were rife, evocations of the Devil and pacts with him were frequent. Who would dream of doing such things in our day, when the religious mania has, to a very large extent, abated? Many obscene expressions of lust may have, in part at least, very much the same origins as the old evocations of the Devil. Henry III of France was forever shuttling back and forth between rites of religious asceticism and offences against nature. He is just the type of a very large class of individuals. In our day, the very countries that lay greatest stress on purity reveal the worst cases of obscenities. Whenever the worship of Cythera is banned, the rites of Sodom and Lesbos come into vogue. The residue is constant. If its natural forms are interfered with, it assumes others.

. . . . .

1334. The sex residue figures actively in the vastly larger portion of literature. Tragedies, comedies, poems, novels, can hardly do without it. Moderns draw a distinction—along what lines is not quite clear—between a literature that is allegedly "moral" and a literature that is allegedly "immoral." The drawing of it oftentimes is a mere matter of hypocrisy, people shrinking at the word and not at the thing, and doing the thing but avoiding the word. At any rate, if it is not actually impossible to write an entertaining novel, comedy, or tragedy without the love-interest, successful ones in which love does not figure to some extent are as rare as white blackbirds—and that is enough to show the tremendous power of the sex residue. The public crowds in throngs to the criminal courts to listen to trials where passions are at issue and attention is the more greedy, the more obscene the matters discussed. Such audiences count no end of men, and especially women, who in other places are energetic defenders of morality and wage frantic war on immorality.

3

The Derivations

1397. We now come to derivations. . . . They account for the production and acceptance of certain theories, so these we shall now be considering from the "subjective" standpoint. We have already come upon derivations in large numbers, though we have not always used that term for them. We shall continue to find them whenever we centre our attention on the ways in which people try to dissemble, change, explain, the real character of this or that mode of conduct. Human beings are persuaded in the main by sentiments (residues), and we may therefore foresee, as for that matter experience shows, that derivations derive the force they have, not, or at least not exclusively, from logico-experimental considerations, but from sentiments. The principal nucleus in a derivative (a non-logico-experimental theory) is a residue, or a number of residues, and around it other secondary residues cluster. That group is produced, and once produced is consolidated, by a powerful force: the need that the human being feels for logical or pseudological developments and which manifests itself in residues of the I-ϵ type. It is in those residues therefore in combination with others that derivations in general originate.

. . . . .

1402. . . . The person who is influenced by a derivation imagines that he accepts or rejects it on logico-experimental grounds. He does not notice that he ordinarily makes up his mind in deference to sentiments and that the accord (or conflict) of two derivations is an accord (or conflict) of residues. When, then, a person sets out to study social phenomena, he halts at manifestations of social activity, that is to say, at derivations, and does not carry his inquiry into the causes of the activity, that is to say, into residues. So it has

80

come about that the history of social institutions has been a history
of derivations, and oftentimes the history of mere patter. The history
of theologies has been offered as the history of religions; the history
of ethical theories, as the history of morals; the history of political
theories, as the history of political institutions. Metaphysics moreover
has supplied all such theories with absolute elements, from which
it was thought that conclusions no less absolute could be drawn by
pure logic. So the history of the theories has become the history of
the deviations observable in the concrete from certain ideal types
existing in the mind of this or that thinker. Not so long ago, some
few scholars sensed that that procedure was taking them far afield
from realities, and to get back to the real, they replaced such abstract
"thinking" with a search for "origins," but without noticing that in
so doing they were merely replacing one metaphysics with another,
explaining the better known by the less known, and facts susceptible
of direct observation by fancies which, for the simple reason that
they related to times very remote, could not be proved; and meantime adding on their own account principles, such as unitary
evolution, that altogether transcended experience.

1403. Derivations, in a word, are things that everybody uses. But
the writers of whom we are thinking ascribe an intrinsic value to
derivations and regard them as functioning directly as determinants
of the social equilibrium. For us, in these volumes, they figure only
as manifestations, as indications, of other forces that are the forces
which really determine the social equilibrium. Very very often, hith-
erto, the social sciences have been theories made up of residues
and derivations and furthermore holding in view the practical purpose of persuading people to act in this or that manner deemed
beneficial to society. [We] . . . aim instead at bringing the social
sciences wholly within the logico-experimental field, quite apart
from any purpose of immediate practical utility, and in the sole
intent of discovering the uniformities that prevail among social
phenomena.

.   .   .   .   .

1400.* Derivations will be differently classified according to the
standpoint from which they are considered. Just here we are thinking of the subjective character of the "explanations" that are given,
through derivations, of certain behaviour, certain ways of thinking;

* This section has been shifted here so that it can immediately precede the
classification it explains (§1419).—J.L.

and of the persuasive force of such explanations. We shall therefore classify derivations according to the character of the explanation. Where there is no explaining there is no derivation; but the moment an explanation is given or sought, a derivation comes into play. The animal does not reason, it acts exclusively by instinct. It uses no derivations therefore. The human being, however, wants to think, and he also feels impelled to keep his instincts and sentiments hidden from view. Rarely, in consequence, is at least a germ of derivation missing in human thinking, just as residues are rarely missing. Residues and derivations can be detected every time we look at a theory or argument that is not strictly logico-experimental. . . . [In] its simplest form, the pure precept, with no explanation or demonstration offered . . . , [it] is the type of argument used by the child or the illiterate in the tautology: "We do thus and so *because* we do thus and so." Such a statement is a pure expression of residues of sociality (Class IV). It really means: "I do as I do (or others do as they do) because that is what is usually done in our community." Then comes a derivation somewhat more complex in that a show is made of accounting for the custom, and one says: "We do thus and so because that is what one *ought* to do." Such derivations are simple assertions. Let us put them in a class by themselves, Class I. But already in the second of the derivations mentioned an indefinite, somewhat mysterious entity, "duty," has put in an appearance. That is our first intimation as to a general manner in which derivations are elaborated: by appealing, that is, under one term or another, to various kinds of sentiments. But going on from there, people are not long satisfied with mere names such as "duty." They want something more concrete, and they also want somehow to account for their using the name. What in the world is this thing "duty" that has suddenly popped up? Everybody has his answer—the illiterate, the educated man, the philosopher, all alike; and we go from the childish answer of the plain man to the abtruse, but from the logico-experimental standpoint no better, theory of the metaphysicist. A first step is taken by appealing to the authority of maxims current in the community that happens to be involved, to the authority of individuals, and, with new elaborations, to the authority of supernatural beings or personifications that feel and act like human beings. That gives us another variety, Class II. The thinking now grows more complicated: it becomes abstruse, abstract, as interpretations of sentiments, abstract entities, and the will of supernatural beings are introduced. That procedure may yield long long sequences of logical or pseudo-logical inferences and eventuate in theories that have the look of scientific theories. Among them are to be counted theologies and systems of metaphysics. Suppose we put them in a Class III. But we have still not exhausted our supply of derivations. Still remaining is a large class where we find proofs that are primarily verbal, explanations that are purely formal but pretend to pass as substantial—Class IV.

. . . . .

1419. Classification of Derivations

CLASS I: ASSERTION

I-α. Assertions of facts, experimental or imaginary
I-β. Assertions of sentiments
I-γ. Mixtures of fact and sentiment

CLASS II: AUTHORITY

II-α. Of one individual or a number of individuals
II-β. Of tradition, usages, and customs
II-γ. Of divine beings, or personifications

CLASS III: ACCORDS WITH SENTIMENTS OR PRINCIPLES

III-α. Accord with sentiments
III-β. Accord with individual interest
III-γ. Accord with collective interest
III-δ. Accord with juridical entities
III-ε. Accord with metaphysical entities
III-ζ. Accord with supernatural entities

CLASS IV: VERBAL PROOFS

IV-α. Indefinite terms designating real things; indefinite things corresponding to terms
IV-β. Terms designating things and arousing incidental sentiments, or incidental sentiments determining choice of terms
IV-γ. Terms with numbers of meanings, and different things designated by single terms
IV-δ. Metaphors, allegories, analogies
IV-ε. Vague, indefinite terms corresponding to nothing concrete

1420. Class I: *Assertion.* This class comprises simple narrations, assertions of fact, assertions by accord of sentiments. They are offered not as such, but in an absolute, axiomatic, dogmatic manner. They may be mere narrations or indications of experimental uniformities; but they are often so worded that it is not clear whether they are mere statements of experimental fact, or expressions of sentiment, or somewhat of both. In many cases, however, their composition may, to a certain degree of probability, be determined. Take the collection of maxims by Publilius Syrus. The first four are of the I-α type: "We mortal men are equally nigh unto death." "Expect from another what you have done to another." "Extinguish with tears the wrath of him who loves you." "To quarrel with a drunken man is to quarrel with one absent." Then comes a maxim of the I-β type: "It is better to receive a wrong than to inflict one." Then come four maxims again of the I-α type, and one of the I-β: "He who loves his wife licentiously is an adulterer." Finally a maxim of the I-γ type: "We all ask, 'Is he rich?' No one asks, 'Is he good?'" That maxim contains an assertion of fact (I-α) and a censure of the fact (I-β). Or further, consider the maxims of Menander: "It is agreeable to pluck everything in its season" (I-α). "Neither do nor learn aught that is shameful" (I-β). "Silence is an ornament to all women" (I-γ).

. . . . .

1434. Class II: *Authority.* Here we get a tool of proof and a tool of persuasion. . . . Here our more particular interest is in authority as an instrument of persuasion. The various derivations in this class are the simplest next after assertions (Class I). As in many other derivations, the residues that are used for purposes of deriving are residues of group-persistence (Class II), II-ζ residues that represent sentiments as objective realities being supported by residues of other kinds, as, for instance, II-β residues (surviving authority of a dead parent, or of the forefathers), residues of tradition (II-α); of persisting uniformities (II-ε), and so on. As a rule Class I residues sooner or later come into play to elongate and complicate the derivation.

1435. II-α: *Authority of one individual or of a number of individuals.* An extreme case would be the derivation that is strictly logical. It is evident that in a given connexion the opinion of an expert has a greater probability of being verified by experience than the opinion of a person who is ignorant of the matters in hand or but slightly acquainted with them. That is a purely logico-experimental situation and we need not linger on it. But there are other kinds of derivations in which the individual's competence is not experimental. It may be assumed to exist from misleading evidence or be altogether fictitious. In the case least remote from the logico-experimental situation the authority is presumed on grounds that may or may not be sound, it being a question of a greater or lesser degree of probability. Next to that would come the case where the competence is stretched, through sentiments of group-persistence, beyond the limits within which it is experimentally valid. The situation dealt with in the familiar maxim, "Cobbler, stick to your last"—*Sutor, ne ultra crepidam*—is of all times and places.

1436. Because he is a first-class politician, Theodore Roosevelt is sure that he also knows history; and he makes bold to deliver a lecture in Berlin in which he makes brilliant display of his perfect ignorance of Greek and Roman history. The university that once listened to the lectures of Mommsen confers on him the title of Doctor *honoris causa*. He makes the discovery—and it is a feat indeed—that the apothegm, *Si vis pacem, para bellum*, is George Washington's—and he becomes a corresponding member of the French Institute of Moral and Political Sciences. Now indubitably Roosevelt is a past master in the art of manipulating elections. He knows all the ins and outs of publicity. He is not a bad hunter of the white rhinoceros. But how can all that make him competent to advise the English on how to govern Egypt, or the French on the number of children they should have? Undoubtedly political considerations and considerations of rather undignified adulation figured in the honours that were conferred upon Roosevelt by the French Institute and the universities of Berlin and Cambridge, to say nothing of flattery which he received from influential statesmen in the course of his rapid flight through Europe. But even where those considerations were not operative there was plenty of admiration for Roosevelt's fatuous chatter. The feeling was that there was a man who was man enough to get himself elected to the presidency of the United States and to make a terrible noise in that office, and that therefore he must surely be competent in any matter relating to the historical and social sciences. It was the feeling also that a man who is competent in one thing is competent in everything; along with a sentiment of generic admiration, which prevents people from distinguishing the respects in which a man is competent from the respects in which he is not.

In a day gone by the prestige of the poet intruded upon every field of human activity, in many cases with some slight logico-experimental justification, since the poet was often a scholar. That consideration no longer applies to the poets and *literati* of our time. Yet in many cases such men are reputed authorities in matters altogether stranger to them. Here is a Brieux, who "solves" some "social question" for us in every one of his dramatic productions. He "discovers" a thesis that has been a commonplace from times most ancient and in the footsteps of Plutarch and Rousseau solemnly tells mothers that they ought to suckle their children. That wins him loud applause from hosts of men and women of no great brains. Anatole France is a novelist of the very first rank, a great stylist, and a master of literary form. He has written in marvellous language novels distinguished for a keen psychological insight and sagacious irony. In all such connexions his authority is not to be disputed. And then, one fine day, he takes it into his head to extend that authority to matters about which he knows much less. He sets out to solve questions of politics, economics, religion, history: he becomes Dreyfusard, Socialist, theologian, historian; and people flock in throngs to him in all of those varied metamorphoses. . . .

1437. The residue of veneration often contributes to lending weight to assertions. The sentiment may show varying degrees of intensity, running from simple admiration to deification outright. It serves for purposes of derivation in all its forms, but in the higher reaches it often appears as authority of verbal or written tradition.

. . . . .

1464. Class III: *Accords with sentiments or principles.* Oftentimes the accord is with the sentiments of the persons producing or accepting the derivation and merely that, but it is represented as an accord with the sentiments of all men, the majority of men, all good men, and so on. Such sentiments eventually become detached from the subject experiencing them and stand as principles.

1465. III-*a*: *Accord with sentiments* (of a larger or smaller number of persons). . . .

1466. The accord with sentiments may arise in three manners, as was the case with deference to authority: 1. An individual may make his conduct conform with the sentiments, real or assumed, of human beings, or of mind in the abstract ("the mind"), out of simple reverence for the opinion of the majority or of experts who are spokesmen for "the mind." That gives us derivations of the III-*a* variety. 2. Or an individual may act as he acts out of fear of harmful consequence to himself or others; and so we get derivations of our III-β, III-γ, III-δ types (accord with individual interest; collective interest; legal principles). 3. Or finally an individual may be impelled to such conformity by a mysterious force—in an extreme case there is an "imperative" operating through occult powers of its own. That gives derivations of our III-ϵ and III-ζ types (accords with metaphysical and supernatural entities). Prominent here among the residues used for purposes of derivation are the residues of sociality (Class IV).

. . . . .

1468. In concrete cases the three attitudes . . . are often combined; but the second (fear of consequences), which is very important when divine personifications are involved, is often barely perceptible or entirely missing in derivations by accord of sentiment, especially in those of the metaphysical type. Furthermore, in many derivations by accord of sentiments one notes a compact group of sociality residues (Class IV), sentiments of reverence for the community on the individual's part, a tendency to imitate, and so on. In that powerful aggregate lies the great sentimental force that impels people to accept opinions which enjoy the consensus of "the majority," or of "all" men.

1469. The accord of sentiments often stands by itself, no explicit attempt being made to give an exact definition to the relationship in which it stands towards objective reality. It is for metaphysics to find that exact definition, and it often takes the form of an assertion that the accord in ideas is identical with an accord in the objects corresponding. The contention more or less is that "if a notion exists in the minds of all men, or of the majority of men, or in mind in the abstract (in 'the mind'), it necessarily corresponds to an objective reality." Often, however, that is not stated—it is tacitly taken for granted: in other words it is left implicit, not made explicit, no verbal form being given to the II-ζ residue to which it corresponds. Sometimes it is stated, now in one form, now in another, as something that is evident or axiomatic—a favourite method with metaphysicists. Then again a show of proof will be given for it, so lengthening the derivation. It will be said, for instance, that what exists in every human mind was put there by God and must therefore necessarily correspond to an objective reality. That is the favourite procedure of theologians, though it is used by other thinkers too. Then there is the very pretty theory of "reminiscence," and no end of metaphysical theories of the same sort.

. . . . .

1510. III-ϵ: *Accord with metaphysical entities.* In derivations of this type accords with certain entities foreign to the experimental domain are sought. As regards substance, an accord of sentiments, a combination of residues, is at work. The form however is supplied by the entities in question, and, without being supernatural, they are non-experimental. The residues used for purposes of derivation come chiefly from our II-δ (persisting abstractions), II-ϵ (persisting uniformities), II-θ (new abstractions) varieties, as usual combining in concrete cases with other residues. From the logico-experimental standpoint there is little or no difference between these derivations and derivations utilizing personified divinities (III-ζ).

1511. Metaphysical derivations are primarily designed for the use and consumption of educated people. The plain man, in our Western countries at least, is tending to revert from such abstractions to personifications. It would of course be absurd to imagine that any of our contemporaries picture "solidarity" as a beautiful woman, the way the Athenians thought of the goddess Athena. All the same, in the minds of our masses such entities as "Solidarity," "Progress," "Humanity," "Democracy," are far from standing on a par with pure abstractions such as a geometric surface, chemical affinity, or luminous ether. They abide in a far loftier realm. They are powerful entities that can work miracles for the good of mankind.

. . . . .

1514. Famous a metaphysical entity that was imagined by Kant and is still admired by many good souls. It is called the *categorical imperative,* and there are plenty of people who pretend to know what it is, though they can never make it clear to anyone who insists on remaining in touch with reality. Kant's formula reconciles, as usual, the egoistic with the altruistic principle, which is here represented by "universal law," a notion pleasantly coddling to sentiments of equality, sociality, and democracy. Many people have accepted Kant's formula in order to retain their customary morality and yet be free of the necessity of having it dependent upon a personified deity. That morality may be made to depend upon Jupiter, upon the God of the Christians, upon the God of Mohammed, upon the will of that estimable demoiselle Milady Nature, or upon *Seine Hoheit* the Categorical Imperative of Kant. Whatever it is, it is all the same thing. Kant gives still another form to his phrase, to wit: "Act as if the maxim of your conduct were to become, by your will, a universal law of nature." A customary trait in all such formulae is that they are so vague in meaning that one can get out of them anything one chooses. And for that reason it would have been a great saving of breath to say, "Act in a way pleasing to Kant or his disciples," for "universal law" will in the end be dispensed with anyhow.

1515. The first question that comes into one's mind as one tries to get some definite meaning into the terms of Kant's formula is whether: (1) the "universal law" is dependent upon some condition; or (2) whether it is unrestricted by any condition of any kind. In other words, can the law be stated in either of the following ways? 1. Every individual who has the traits M ought to act in a certain manner. 2. Every individual, regardless of his traits, ought to act in a certain manner.

1516. If the first form of statement be adopted, the law itself means nothing, and the problem then is to determine which traits M it is permissible to consider; for if the choice of traits is left to the person who is to observe the law, he will always find a way to select traits that will allow him to do exactly as he chooses without violating the law. If he wants to justify slavery, he will say with Aristotle that some men are born to command (among them, of course, the gentleman who is interpreting the law) and other men are born to obey. If he wants to steal, he will say that it may very well be a universal law that he who has less should take from him who has more. If he wants to kill an enemy he will say that revenge can easily be a universal law; and so on.

1517. To judge by the first application that Kant makes of his principle, he would seem to reject that interpretation. Making no distinctions between individuals, he concludes that suicide could not be a universal law of nature. [Kant, *Metaphysik der Sitten*.]

1518. So let us look at the second interpretation (where no distinctions or limitations in individuals are recognized). Kant's reasoning might seem able to stand after a fashion. But there is another trouble with it. Before it could stand, the whole human race would have to constitute one homogeneous mass, without the least differentiation in the functions of individuals. If distinctions are admitted, it is possible for some men to command and others to obey; but not if distinctions are not admitted, for there can be no universal law that all men should command and no one obey. A man wants to spend his life studying mathematics. If distinctions are in order, he may do so without violating the Kantian law, since it may well be a universal law that a person possessing certain traits M should spend his life studying mathematics, and that a person not possessing those traits should till the soil or otherwise employ himself. But if distinctions are not allowed, if, as in the case of the suicide, one refuses to divide individuals into classes, there can be no universal law that all men should spend their lives studying mathematics, if for no other reason, for the very good one that they would starve; and therefore *no one* could be allowed to spend his life in such mathematical studies.

Such implications are not noticed, because people reason on sentiments and not with the facts before their eyes.

1519. As metaphysicists habitually do, after giving what he says is to be a single principle, Kant begins filling out with other principles, which come bobbing up no one knows from where. In a third case that he considers, *Op. cit.*, p. 49 (Semple, pp. 35–36), still "a third [person] finds himself possessed of certain powers of mind [Those are qualifications, conditions. Why were they not mentioned in the case of the presumptive suicide? Why was it not said in his case, "A person finds himself possessed of a certain nature whereby life for him is a painful burden and not a pleasure"?] which, with some slight culture, might render him a highly useful member of society; but he is in easy circumstances and prefers amusement to the thankless toil of cultivating his understanding and perfecting his nature." (Semple translation.) He wants to know whether the latter can be a universal law. The answer is in the affirmative, at least from a certain point of view: "He observes that [such] an order of things might continue to exist under a law enjoining men to let their talents rust (after the manner of a South Sea Islander) and to devote their lives to amusement." It would seem, then, if one would adhere strictly to the formula which Kant has posited as a single comprehensive principle, that since such a course of action can be a universal law, it should be permissible. But not so! "It is impossible for any one *to will* that such should become a universal law of nature, or were by an instinct implanted in his system [The formula does not mention any such "instinct."]; for he, as [an] Intelligent [being], of necessity wills all his faculties to become developed, such being given him in order that they may subserve his various and manifold ends and purposes." (Semple translation.) Here we have a principle altogether new: that certain things are given us (no one knows by whom) for certain ends and purposes.

In order to reason in that fashion one would have to modify the terms in Kant's formula and say: "Act only on a maxim that it would be your will at the same time to have become a universal law. However, do not let yourself be deceived by the possessive 'your.' To say 'your will' is just my way of saying. In reality it is something that must necessarily exist in a man, full account being taken of the capacities with which he is endowed, of his designs and purposes, and of many other fine things that will be explained to you at the proper time and place." That much granted, one might just as well, from the logico-experimental standpoint, do away with "will" altogether, for it is thrown overboard in any event. But not so from the standpoint of sentiment. The appeal to "will" serves its purpose in flattering egoistic sentiments and giving hearer or reader the satisfaction of having it reconciled with his sentiments of altruism. And other sentiments also are stirred by the maxim of "universal law": first, a feeling of satisfaction that there should be an absolute norm which is superior to captious wranglings and petty human altercations—something established by Nature; and then that sum of sentiments whereby we vaguely sense the utility of the principle that the decisions of judges should be based on reasons, on general rules, and that laws also should be made with reference to such rules and not against or in favour of any given individual.

1520. The utility, we may note in passing, is really there, for such general rules do, in spite of everything, serve as a check on mere whim, just as Kant's law itself does. But the gain is not after all so very great; for if he chooses, a judge can always find a way to give a semblance of generality to a partisan decision. If, as between three persons, A, B, and C, one is concerned to favour or to harm A, one seeks, and one always finds, some aspect wherein A is different from B and C, and the decision is based on that aspect and therefore given an appearance of generality. That is saying nothing of that much-followed method of deciding in general and applying in particular, now with, now without, indulgence. So all our codes contain a law that, in the general, punishes assaults and batteries. But in the particular, the courts shut one eye, and even two, in cases of assaults and batteries committed by strikers on non-unionized workers. In Italy, before the war of 1911 it was possible to insult an army officer without interference from the courts. A certain Deputy was able to slander an army officer on purely private grounds that had nothing to do with politics; and though he was convicted in a criminal court he did not spend a day in prison even after he had failed of re-election to the parliament. Then the war with Turkey came and the pendulum swung to the other extreme. At the Scala Opera House in Milan individuals were abused and beaten with impunity for mere failure to rise to their feet when the "Royal March" was being played.

. . . . .

1543. Class IV: Verbal proofs. This class is made up of verbal derivations obtained through the use of terms of indefinite, doubtful, equivocal meaning and which do not correspond to any reality. If the classification were to be taken in a very loose sense, it would embrace nearly all derivations, and nothing would be gained by distinguishing Class IV derivations from the others. The definition must therefore be taken as applying to cases in which the verbal character of the derivation is very conspicuous, prevailing over other traits. In this class logical sophistries may be conveniently placed as regards their purely formal element, so far, that is, as they serve to satisfy the need of logical development that human beings feel (residues I-ϵ). But that element is nearly always incidental and does not determine the judgment of the person who accepts the derivation. The judgment results from an element of far greater importance— the sentiments that are stirred by the reasoning. Ordinarily such logical sophistries deceive no one who is not already disposed to be deceived. More exactly, there is no deception at all. The author of the argument and those who accept it are already in mutual agreement in virtue of an accord of sentiments, which they are merely supplementing, for good measure, with the dressing of the logical sophistry.

1544. The residues chiefly utilized for purposes of derivation in verbal proofs are the residues of our II-ζ variety. They give body to an abstraction that has a name, endowing it with reality because it has a name. They also assume, vice versa, that a name necessarily has some real thing corresponding to it. Others of our Class II residues also figure, as well as residues of the I-γ type (mysterious linkings of names and things). In the special case still other residues may be involved. The residues indicate the desire to attain certain ends. That desire is humoured by a number of devices which language readily makes available.

1545. As we have time and again noted, the terms of ordinary parlance do not, in general, correspond to sharply defined things, and therefore all arguments in which such terms are used run the risk of being nothing but verbal derivations. There is least danger of that in scientific reasonings, for in such cases the thinker always has before his mind the things for which his terms are mere designations, mere labels. The danger is greater in derivations where the terms begin by not being just labels, and so on and on progressively till we get to metaphysical derivations, which are almost never wanting in the traits of the verbal derivation.

1546. When a term that can have more than one meaning is used in a syllogism, the syllogism may come to have more than three terms and so be fallacious. Very often it is the middle term that vitiates the syllogism by its indefiniteness. Such derivations vary from one extreme, where there is a simple play on words that no one takes seriously, to another extreme where a reasoning seems profound precisely because of its obscurity and indefiniteness. Take the argument, $A = X$, $X = B$, therefore $A = B$. If X has two meanings that cannot possibly be confused—for instance, the bark of a tree and the bark of a dog—we get a mere pun. But if X designates a fairly large and fairly vague aggregate of sentiments, certain sentiments prevail in the proposition, $A = X$, and certain other sentiments in the proposition, $X = B$. In reality, therefore, X is two different things: but people do not notice that and applaud the argument. If X is "Nature," "Right Reason," "the Good," or something else of that sort, one may be almost certain, not to say certain, that the argument is of the verbal type. Example: "One lives well according to Nature. Nature recognizes no private property. Therefore one lives well without private property." In the first proposition, the term "Nature" designates a vague sum of sentiments, distinguishes something that is in accord with our inclinations (what is "natural" to us) from something that we do only under compulsion (from what is foreign or repugnant to us), and instinctively we assent to the proposition that "one lives well according to Nature." The second proposition brings to the fore sentiments that distinguish things which the human being does (artificial things) from things that exist independently of human action (things that

are "natural"); and there again the person following the lead of his
sentiments will admit that private property is not a product of Nature, that Nature does not recognize it. Put the two propositions
together and it logically follows that "one lives well without private
property"; and if this proposition chances to harmonize with the
sentiments of the person at whom the argument is directed, he will
regard it as sound from every point of view. And perfect it is in the
sense of humouring all the desires of the person who hears it, including his desire for a logical tinting—for some derivation or other.

1547. In concrete cases the Class IV derivations that we are here
dividing into subvarieties are used together, and often also in combination with other derivations. Only by abstraction can we isolate
the simple derivations of which the concrete derivation is com-
pounded. That point must never be forgotten.

1548. The subgenera in Class IV show derivations of two forms:
in the first, procedure is from the thing to the term, in the second,
from the term to the thing, real or imaginary as the thing may be.
In concrete cases the two forms often mingle: after going from the
thing to the term, one goes back from the term to something else.
There are plenty of arguments that amount, substantially, to nothing more than that.

· · · · ·

4

Properties of Residues
and Derivations

1687. The examination of residues and derivations that we have just completed has acquainted us with the manifestations of certain forces which influence human society and consequently with those forces themselves. So step by step we are gradually approaching our goal, which has been to discover the form that society assumes in virtue of the forces acting upon it. The road is a long one, but there is no way of shortening it if we insist on accepting no guides but the facts. We have identified and classified residues and derivations and in so doing we have also learned something about their properties. The time has now come to go into the matter of their properties in detail.*

. . . . .

1690. Returning to the matter of our modes of expression, . . . note that since sentiments are manifested by residues we shall often, for the sake of brevity, use the word "residues" as including the sentiments that they manifest. So we shall say, simply, that residues are among the elements which determine the social equilibrium, a statement that must be translated and understood as meaning that "the sentiments manifested by residues are among the elements which stand toward the social equilibrium in a relationship of reciprocal determination." But that statement too is elliptical and has again to be translated. Let us beware of ascribing any objective existence to our residues or even to sentiments. What we observe in reality is a group of human beings in a mental condition indicated

* This paragraph is actually a footnote to §1687. I find it very convenient as part of the text—J. L.

by what we call sentiments. Our proposition must, therefore, be translated in the following terms: "The mental states that are indicated by the sentiments expressed in residues are among the elements that stand in a relation of reciprocal determination with the social equilibrium." But if we would express ourselves in a language altogether exact, that is still not enough. What in the world are those "mental states" or, if one will, those "psychic conditions"? They are abstractions. And what underlies the abstractions? So we are obliged to say: "The actions of human beings are among the elements that stand in a relationship of reciprocal determination with the social equilibrium. Among such actions are certain manifestations that we designate by the term "residues" and which are closely correlated with other acts so that once we know the residues we may, under certain circumstances, know the actions. Therefore we shall say that residues are among the elements that stand in a relation of reciprocal determination with the social equilibrium."

It is well enough to say all that once, just to fix with strict exactness the meaning of the terms we use; but it would be useless, tiresome, and altogether pedantic to be for ever talking with such prolixity. That is why we replace the proposition just stated with its shorter original form: "Residues are among the elements that determine the social equilibrium." [1]

Derivations also manifest sentiments. Directly, they manifest the sentiments that correspond to the residues in which they originate. Indirectly they manifest sentiments through the residues that serve for purposes of derivation. But to speak of derivations in place of the residues they manifest, as is done in ordinary parlance, might lead to serious misapprehensions, and we shall refrain from doing so in all cases where any doubt as to the meaning of a statement is possible.

The subject being very important, it will not come amiss to offer some further elucidation. We observe, for example, a number of cases in which a hen defends her chicks, and we epitomize our observation of past facts, our forecast of future facts, and our guess at a uniformity, by saying that "the hen defends her chicks," that

---

[1] Nor can the short cut result in any harm if attention is paid to the exact sense we give to the terms we use. In the same way pure economics uses the term "ophelimity" and mechanics the term "force," which, in their relations to the economic and mechanical equilibria respectively, correspond to the term "sentiment" ("residue") in its relations to the social equilibrium. . . . .

present in the hen is a sentiment that prompts her to defend her chicks, that that defence is the consequence of a given psychic state. So we observe a number of cases in which certain individuals sacrifice their lives for their countries; and we epitomize our observation of the past fact, our forecast of future fact, and our conception of a uniformity embracing large numbers of individuals, by saying that "Human beings—or some human beings—sacrifice their lives for their countries," that present in them is a sentiment which prompts them to sacrifice their lives for their countries, that such sacrifice is the consequence of a given psychic state.

But in human beings we further observe certain facts that are a consequence of their using language and are therefore not observable in animals: human beings, that is, express in language certain things which we associate with the facts that are observable when they sacrifice their lives for their countries. They say, for instance, "Dulce et decorum est pro patria mori"; and we say that they express in that way a certain sentiment, a certain psychic state, and so on. But that is not very exact, for the propositions that we take as expressions of a sentiment (or better, of a sum of sentiments), a psychic state, and so on, are multiple and diverse. It was by separating in them elements that are constant from variable elements that we got residues and derivations and said that the residue expresses that sentiment, that psychic state, and so on. But in so saying we are adding something to the facts. All that experimental observation shows is a set of simultaneous facts—men dying for their countries and using certain modes of speech. We may state that situation in the following propositions, which start close to reality and gradually get farther and farther away from it: 1. Observable side by side are acts of self-sacrifice for country and expressions of approval or praise for such acts. Such expressions have an element in common. We call it a residue. 2. Human beings sacrifice themselves for country and have a sentiment, manifested by residues, which spurs them to such conduct. The divergence from reality lies in the term "sentiment," which has an element of vagueness. Then again, the uniformity is stated without limitations, whereas some limitation is essential. Finally, even the assumption that conduct is always inspired by sentiment is open to question. 3. Instead of saying, "and have a sentiment . . .", the form is, "because they have a sentiment. . . ." The term "because" takes us still farther away from reality, in that it asserts a relationship of cause and effect, and we have no certain knowledge that any such relation exists. 4. Human beings *believe* it their duty to sacrifice themselves for country; *therefore they sacrifice themselves.* . . . In that we get very very far from reality, assuming that the conduct is the consequence of certain beliefs and so substituting logical for non-logical conduct. This fourth manner of statement is the usual one, but it easily leads astray, even if we bear in mind that it is only another form for 1. There is no objection to the use of 2, provided we bear in mind that, strictly speaking, we are always to check it by reference to 1.² The third manner, 3, is also serviceable; but we must always remember that it really stands for 1, and be on our guard against drawing logical inferences from the term "because" that appears in it. The terms "sentiments," "residues," and so on, are convenient makeshifts in sociology, just as the term "force" has proved convenient in mechanics. They may be used without untoward results if the realities to which they correspond are always kept clearly in mind.

1691. *Residues in general.* In identifying and classifying residues we considered them without regard to the intensity of the sentiments that are manifested through them and independently of the number of persons in whom they are to be met with. In other words, we dissevered them by a process of abstraction from the concrete individuals to whom they belong. We must now take account of all such circumstances.

Suppose, first of all, we consider the matter of intensities. It is important to distinguish between the intensity proper of a residue and the intensity that it derives from the general tendency of the individual to be more or less energetic. A person may have a strong sense of patriotism but still be a physical coward. In that case he will fight less effectively for his country than a man whose patriotism is much less virulent but who is a man of courage. If a person has a strong combination-instinct, but is inclined to indolence, he will utilize fewer combinations than a person in whom that instinct is not so strong but who is inclined to be active. We may therefore conclude that certain circumstances which we may designate by the term "strength," or its opposite "weakness," raise or lower the general level of this or that residue.

1692. Then suppose we look at residues with respect to the concrete individuals to whom they belong. . . .

---

² In point of fact, we have used form 2 freely in this work and shall continue to do so, especially in an equivalent variant relating conduct and residues.

1693. Under a static aspect, we must consider: (1) The distribution of residues in a given society; and (2) their distribution in the different strata in that society. From a dynamic point of view we have to see: (1) how, approximately, residues vary in time, whether as a result of changes in the individuals belonging to one same social stratum, or of changes caused by a mixing of social strata; and (2) how each of those two things arises.

1694. Due attention must be paid, moreover, to the rhythmical movement that is observable in all social phenomena. A phenomenon that is virtually constant is not represented by a straight line, *mn* (Figure 3), but by an undulating curve, *svt*. A phenomenon of in-

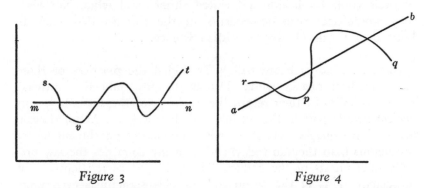

Figure 3   Figure 4

creasing intensity (Figure 4) is represented not by a straight line, *ab*, but by an undulating curve, *rpq*. Lines such as *mn* and *ab* represent the *mean movement* of the phenomenon, and that movement we now propose to examine.

1695. *Distribution and change in society as a whole.* We are not here inquiring as to the causes that determine the character of a society—whether race, climate, geographical situation, fertility of soil, possibilities of economic productivity, or the like. We are looking at historical societies as fact, without any concern, for the present, with origins. Observable in such historical societies are phenomena that vary little in substance, but widely in forms. As the various religions succeed one another in history, their forms may be as different as one please, but after all they are all expressions of religious sentiments that vary but slightly. The same may be said of the various forms of government, each of which explicitly or implicitly has its own "divine right." The modern free-thinker enforces, in the name of Science, Holy of Holies, a morality but slightly differing from the code that the God of the Israelites proclaimed for His people, or the code that the Christians received from their God; or the codes that now one, now another, of the ancient peoples received from gods or from lawgivers legendary or divine. Nor is there any very appreciable difference, either, in the derivations by which the imperative and absolute character of all such ethical systems is justified.

Similar uniformities are observable even in phenomena much less important. In ancient times people who were sick made pilgrimages to the temples of Aesculapius in order to regain their health. They were succeeded in the Middle Ages by devout Christians who prayed to their saints for health and visited shrines and relics. Nowadays they would recognize descendants in the throngs that flock to Lourdes, in the devotees of "Christian Science. . . ."

. . . . .

1697. . . . To such are still to be added the practices of those many medical quacks whom Daudet happily dubbed "deathers" ("*morticoles*"). In their regard the credulity of the ancients has its perfect counterpart in the credulity of the moderns. At no time in history have quacks flourished more abundantly on the money of simpletons than they do today; and in many countries the law protects such priests of the goddess "Science" just as religiously as it protected priests of the pagan gods of old—sometimes even more so. Believers gather in droves in those clinics and sanitoria which are the temples of the modern quack. Some of them get well, if Mother Nature chances to look upon them with kindly eye; but all of them contribute to the collection-box of the high-priests of the goddess "Science" and their acolytes—among whom, let us not fail to count the pharmacists who sell their drugs at 1000 per cent profit; and the inventors of those patent medicines which shoot across the sky of publicity like meteors, cure every conceivable disease for more or less extensive, and often very brief, periods of time, and then are gone; not without leaving huge fortunes in the pockets of certain traders on public credulity who exploit the poor in spirit under the kindly eye of the legislator. And there is no argument, no fact, however obvious, however striking, that can avail to open the eyes of the fools who are thus fleeced.

Confessors were accused in days of old of extorting legacies from the dying under threat of eternal punishment. Today our "deathers" go that one better. They get all they can from a patient before he dies, then fleece his heirs by presenting exorbitant bills for services rendered, relying upon the probability that to avoid litigation and suspicion of ingratitude towards the dead the heirs will submit to the blackmail and come forward with the money. . . .

1698. Hosts of other facts of the same sort might be marshalled and all of them go to show that superstitions which might readily be supposed to have vanished long since have in reality merely changed their forms and are still alive under new guises. From the Middle Ages on to our time, the influence of magic on human societies has lessened, even if we reckon in the count its legacies to mind-readings, spiritualisms, telepathies, and other systems of thaumaturgy; but the domain from which it was banished has been partly occupied by the goddess Science. Taken all in all, in the departments of the arts and sciences development has certainly been in the direction of an increase in the importance attached to experimental methods; but the evidence in favour of such an evolution is not so good if we turn to the fields of politics and social organization. It is significant that simple combinations foreign to scientific experience are far from having disappeared from modern social life; in fact, they persist in great numbers, thriving in prosperous exuberance. Since simple combinations, in great part at least, are based on I-δ residues (need for combining residues), it is safe to say that that group of residues as a whole has changed much less than would seem to be the case at first sight.

1699. Then again, experimental science itself originates in the instinct of combinations and corresponds to Class I residues. But that is the one point such science has in common with the vagaries of magic and other fantastic systems. If that fact is overlooked, one might imagine that Class I as a whole had been enormously strengthened in the course of past centuries, cutting in on the domain of Class II residues (group-persistences). Such a strengthening there has certainly been, but closer examination shows that the gain has been smaller than would seem. The combinations of experimental science have been vastly expanding all the way down to our own times, but for the most part they have occupied territory formerly held by the combinations of trial-and-error empiricism, magic, theology, and metaphysics. From the standpoint of social utility that displacement in combinations is very advantageous; but as regards the rôle played by residues in human conduct it is evident that the compensation has been very considerable also, so that the class as a whole has changed much less than the two elements of which it is made up; and considering Class I as a whole, it is apparent that, substantially, it changes but slightly and very slowly.

1700. The same may be said of the other classes of residues. Suppose, for instance, we consider Class II (group-persistences). The II-β variety in that class (relations of living and dead) has by no means disappeared. Indeed it was through observation of present-day phenomena that we were able to strip it clear of the derivations which in former times had hidden it from view. But there can be no doubt that it figures much less extensively in our times than in a remote era, when worship of the dead was virtually the only cult our Graeco-Latin ancestors knew; or in the Middle Ages, when the chief concern of the living seems to have been to endow masses for the dead. We may confidently assert, therefore, that the importance of residues of our II-β variety has greatly diminished in the course of the centuries.

1701. But that falling-off has been balanced, to some extent at least, by intensifications on the part of other varieties in the same class, so that the class as a whole has not greatly changed. The gods of Graeco-Latin polytheism came little by little to occupy the territory left vacant by a waning worship of the dead; and they in their turn were displaced by the divinities and saints of Christianity. In the sixteenth century the Reformation waged bitter war on the cult of relics, and especially on the rites practised in the Roman Church for the mitigation of punishments after death. Yet, at bottom, the Reformation merely replaced the old group-persistences with new ones. Life at Geneva under Calvin was much less free, much more extensively governed by ultra-experimental considerations, than life in Rome ever had been under the rule of the Popes; and taken all in all, Protestantism was much more narrow-minded, much more oppressive, than the Catholic Church had been in countries where the Reform superseded Catholicism; while Catholicism, on its side, under the impact of the attack upon it became less tolerant, less indulgent, more aggressive. In a word, in the days of Leo X and before the day of Luther, Rome enjoyed a freedom of thought and speech which vanished, quite, in Protestant countries and therefore in Catholic countries also. Protestants themselves point out that their Reformation tended to stimulate the "religious spirit." Which is another way of saying that it extended the influence of the Class II residues.

. . . . .

1718. For a given society . . . we may establish the following scale of variations, increasing from the first to the last categories: (1) Classes of residues; (2) the genera in such classes; (3) derivations. A graph (Figure 5) may make the relations between classes

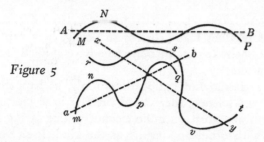

Figure 5

and genera clearer. The movement in time of a class of residues may be represented by the undulating curve *MNP*; certain genera are represented by the curves, also undulatory, *mnpq*, *rsvt*. The waves are smaller for the class than for many of its genera. The mean movement of the class, which, let us say, is in a direction of increase, is represented by *AB*; and the same movement in the genera, some of which are increasing, others diminishing, by *ab*, *xy*. The variation represented by *AB* is much less wide than the variations in some of the genera, *ab*, *xy*. On the whole, there is a certain compensation between genera and it is owing to such compensations that both the variation represented by *AB*, and the amplitude of fluctuation on the curve *MNP*, are attenuated as regards the class as a whole.

As regards social phenomena in general, this undulatory movement creates difficulties that may become quite serious, if one is to gauge the movement of a sentiment, quite apart from occasional, temporary, or incidental fluctuations. If, for example, one should compare the position *r* with the position *s*, to get the general trend of the residue, one would conclude that the sentiment was growing in intensity, whereas the line *xy* shows that, on the average and in general, there is a diminishing intensity. . . . When a development is susceptible of measurement and we have observations extending over long periods of time, it is fairly easy to eliminate such difficulties. By interpolation one may determine the line, *xy*, about which the intensity is fluctuating and so discover its mean general direction. This is much more difficult when accurate measurements for a sentiment are not available or cannot be made, for then we are obliged to replace accurate mathematical quantities with estimates in which arbitrary statement, individual impression, and perhaps even fancy, play a more or less important part. Such estimates must therefore be subjected to the severest examination and no possible verification ignored.

.   .   .   .   .

1719a. . . . If residues really change so slowly, how can the fact have escaped the many talented writers who have studied the various aspects of human society?

The answer is: It did not escape them; only, as happens in the early stages of every science, they stated the fact in vague terms and without aiming at any great scientific exactness. The saying *Nil novi sub sole*, along with other apothegms of the kind, itself voices the perception, more or less veiled by sentiment, that there is something, at least, that is constant in social phenomena. The implicit premise in the pedantry of grammarians who strive to force language forms of past generations upon their contemporaries and younger generations is that sentiments have not changed, and will not change to the point of requiring new language-forms to express them. The groundwork of language does change, but very slowly. Neologisms become unavoidable, but in small numbers. Grammatical forms are modified, but substance endures through the ages. A long line of writers imitated the ancients and some pedants indeed even tried to prescribe that imitation. That would not be understandable unless such persons and the publics they addressed had had sentiments very kindred to those voiced by the ancients. However, quite aside from the matter of imitation, how could we still enjoy the poems of Homer and the elegies, tragedies and comedies of the Greeks and Latins if we did not find them expressing sentiments that, in great part at least, we share? . . . Do we not find in Thucydides, Polybius, Tacitus, and other ancient historians, descriptions of things that reveal, under different, sometimes very different, guises, a fund of human sentiments identical with what we observe today? All thinkers who have pondered social phenomena at all deeply have not seldom been led to detect in them certain elements that are variable and certain others that are relatively stable. All we have been doing in these volumes is to offer a scientific formulation of the concept, just as the chemist who "discovered" aluminium and calcium carbonate was merely giving a scientific formulation to notions that had existed long before him and, in fact, ever since human beings had been able to distinguish between clay and limestone.

. . . . .

1723. *Distribution of residues and change in residues in the various strata of a given society.* Residues are not evenly distributed nor are they of equal intensities in the various strata of a given society. The fact is a commonplace and has been familiar in every age. The neophobia and superstition of the lower classes has often been remarked, and it is a well-known fact of history that they were the last to abandon faith in the religion which derived its very name, paganism ("ruralism"), from them. The residues of widest diffusion and greatest intensity in the uneducated are referable to Classes II and III (activity), whereas the opposite is often the case with the residues of our Class V (individual integrity).

1724. Dividing society into two strata, calling one the "lower" and the other the "higher," brings us one step closer to the concrete than we were in thinking of society as a homogeneous unit, though it still leaves us far enough removed from anything concrete, anything real.

. . . . .

1727. . . . . There is a general recognition that, on the whole, sentiments tend to vary with occupation. Along that line, the so-called theory of economic materialism might be linked up with the theory of residues by correlating residues with economic status; and as far as it goes such a correlation would undoubtedly be sound. It goes wrong, however, in isolating economic status from other social factors, towards which, on the contrary, it stands in a relation of interdependence; and, further, in envisaging a single relation of cause and effect, whereas there are many many such relations all functioning simultaneously.

. . . . .

1732. . . . . There are various ways of envisaging interdependent phenomena. Suppose we classify them: 1. Relations of cause and effect, only, may be considered, and interdependence wholly disregarded. 2. Interdependence may be taken into account: 2a. Relations of cause and effect are still considered, but allowance is made for interdependence by considering actions and reactions, and by other

devices. 2b. One may work directly on the hypothesis of interdependence. The soundest method, undoubtedly, is the one we designate
as 2b, but unfortunately it can be followed in but relatively few cases
because of the conditions that it requires. Essential to it, in fact, is
the use of mathematical logic, which alone can take full account of
interdependencies in the broadest sense. It can be used, therefore,
only for phenomena susceptible of measurement—a limitation that
excludes many many problems, and virtually all the problems peculiar
to sociology. Then again, even when a phenomenon is in itself meas-
urable, serious difficulties arise as soon as it becomes at all complex.
An interesting example of that may be seen in celestial mechanics,
where insuperable difficulties still stand in the way of determining
the movements of many bodies of about equal mass when some of
the interdependencies can no longer be regarded as perturbations.
Pure economics goes so far as to state the equations for certain phenomena, but not so far as to be able to solve them, at least in their
general form. So as regards the economic and social sciences, the 2b
method remains as an ideal goal that is almost never attained in the
concrete. Shall we say, on that account, that it is useless? No, because from it we derive, if nothing more, two great advantages. 1. It
gives us a picture of a situation, which we could get in no other way.
The surface of the Earth does not, to be sure, have the shape of a
geometric sphere; and yet to picture the Earth in that way does help
to give some notion of what the Earth is like. 2. It sign-boards the
path we have to follow if we are to avoid the pitfalls of method 1
and so approximate realities. Even a beacon we shall never reach
may serve to indicate a course. By analogy we can carry over the results achieved by mathematical economics into sociology and so
equip ourselves with concepts that we could get in no other way
and which we can proceed to verify on experience, to decide whether
they are to be kept or thrown away. 3. Finally, the concept of interdependence, imperfect though it be, is a guide to using 2a, which
tries, through use of relations of cause and effect, to produce results
that are at least something like what we would have got by following
2b; and it helps to avoid the errors inherent in 1, which is the least
perfect of the three, the most exposed to error. In our present state
of knowledge the advantages of method 2b are therefore not so much
direct as indirect. That method is a light and a guide to save us
from the pitfalls of 1 and to beckon to a closer approximation of
reality. This is not the place to linger on details of the method 2a.

We will simply note, because the point will be of use to us presently, that the method 2a proves to be workable when we have a principal phenomenon that exactly or approximately assumes the form of a relationship of cause and effect, and then incidental, secondary or less important phenomena with which interdependence arises. When we are able to reduce a situation to that type, which after all is the type of celestial mechanics, we are in a fair way to understand it. With just such a reduction in mind, we saw that residues were much more stable than derivations, and we were therefore able to regard them as in part "causes" of derivations, but without forgetting secondary effects of derivations, which sometimes, be it in subordinate ways, may be "causes" of residues. Now we are seeing that the different social classes show different residues, but for the moment we are not deciding whether it is living in a certain class that produces certain residues in individuals, or whether it is the presence of those residues in those individuals that drives them into that class, or, better yet, whether the two effects may not be there simultaneously. For the present we are to confine ourselves to describing such uniformities as are discernible in the distribution of residues in the various social classes.

1733. Data in abundance are available on that point. They are not very exact, often coming forward under literary or metaphysical guises. From them, nevertheless, we are able to infer with reasonable probability that for the various strata in society the scale of increasing variability noted above (§1718) still holds valid: (1) Classes of residues; (2) the genera of those classes; (3) derivations. But the variability is greater for a given social stratum than for society as a whole, since as regards the latter compensations take place between the various strata. There are, furthermore, social categories comprising few individuals within which variations may be wide and sudden, whereas they are slight and gradual for the mass of the citizenry. The higher classes change styles in dress much more readily than the lower classes. So they change in their sentiments and, even more, in their ways of expressing their sentiments. Changes in style in the various branches of human activity are followed much more closely by the wealthier, or higher, than by the poorer, or lower, classes. Not a few changes, indeed, remain within the confines of the higher classes and often fail to reach the lower because they have disappeared in the higher before reaching the lower.

1734. Unfortunately, history and literature give a better picture of the states of mind, the sentiments, the customs of the few individuals located in the higher strata of society than of those same things in the larger number of individuals belonging to the lower strata. In that fact lies the source of many serious errors. There is a temptation to extend to a whole population, or the larger part of it, traits that are characteristic of a small, perhaps an insignificant, number of individuals. And failure to take account of changes in the composition of the higher classes due to class-circulation leads to the further error of mistaking changes in the personnel of a class for changes in the sentiments of individuals. In a closed class, X, sentiments and expressions of sentiments may change; but if the class X is open, a further change results from changes in the composition of the class; and this second change depends, in its turn, upon the greater or lesser rapidity of the circulation.

5

🙢🙢🙢

The Social System
and Equilibrium

2025. *Heterogeneousness of society and circulation among its various elements.* We have more than once found ourselves called upon to consider the heterogeneous character of society, and we shall have to consider it all the more closely now that we are coming to our investigation of the conditions that determine the social equilibrium. To have a clear road ahead of us, it would be wise to go into that matter somewhat thoroughly at this point.

Whether certain theorists like it or not, the fact is that human society is not a homogeneous thing, that individuals are physically, morally, and intellectually different. Here we are interested in things as they actually are. Of that fact, therefore, we have to take account. And we must also take account of another fact: that the social classes are not entirely distinct, even in countries where a caste system prevails; and that in modern civilized countries circulation among the various classes is exceedingly rapid. To consider at all exhaustively here this matter of the diversity of the vastly numerous social groups and the numberless ways in which they mix is out of the question. As usual, therefore, since we cannot have the more, we must rest content with the less and try to make the problem easier in order to have it the more manageable. That is a first step along a path that others may go on following. We shall consider the problem only in its bearing on the social equilibrium and try to reduce as far as possible the numbers of the groups and the modes of circulation, putting under one head phenomena that prove to be roughly and after a fashion similar.

2026. *Social élites and their circulation.* Suppose we begin by giving a theoretical definition of the thing we are dealing with, making it as exact as possible, and then go on to see what practical considerations we can replace it with to get a first approximation. . . .

2027. Let us assume that in every branch of human activity each individual is given an index which stands as a sign of his capacity, very much the way grades are given in the various subjects in examinations in school. The highest type of lawyer, for instance, will be given 10. The man who does not get a client will be given 1 —reserving zero for the man who is an out-and-out idiot. To the man who has made his millions—honestly or dishonestly as the case may be—we will give 10. To the man who has earned his thousands we will give 6; to such as just manage to keep out of the poor-house, 1, keeping zero for those who get in. To the woman "in politics," such as the Aspasia of Pericles, the Maintenon of Louis XIV, the Pompadour of Louis XV, who has managed to infatuate a man of power and play a part in the man's career, we shall give some higher number, such as 8 or 9; to the strumpet who merely satisfies the senses of such a man and exerts no influence on public affairs, we shall give zero. To a clever rascal who knows how to fool people and still keep clear of the penitentiary, we shall give 8, 9, or 10, according to the number of geese he has plucked and the amount of money he has been able to get out of them. To the sneak-thief who snatches a piece of silver from a restaurant table and runs away into the arms of a policeman, we shall give 1. To a poet like Carducci we shall give 8 or 9 according to our tastes; to a scribbler who puts people to rout with his sonnets we shall give zero. For chess-players we can get very precise indices, noting what matches, and how many, they have won. And so on for all the branches of human activity.

. . . . .

2030. . . . As usual, again, we are replacing imperceptible variations in absolutely exact numbers with the sharp variations corresponding to groupings by class, just as in examinations those who are passed are sharply and arbitrarily distinguished from those who are "failed," and just as in the matter of physical age we distinguish children from young people, the young from the aged.

2031. So let us make a class of the people who have the highest indices in their branch of activity, and to that class give the name of *élite*.

2032. For the particular investigation with which we are engaged, a study of the social equilibrium, it will help if we further divide that class into two classes: a *governing élite*, comprising individuals who directly or indirectly play some considerable part in government, and a *non-governing élite*, comprising the rest.

. . . . .

2034. So we get two strata in a population: (1) A lower stratum, the *non-élite*, with whose possible influence on government we are not just here concerned; then (2) a higher stratum, the *élite*, which is divided into two: (a) a governing *élite*; (b) a non-governing *élite*.

2035. In the concrete, there are no examinations whereby each person is assigned to his proper place in these various classes. That deficiency is made up for by other means, by various sorts of labels that serve the purpose after a fashion. Such labels are the rule even where there are examinations. The label "lawyer" is affixed to a man who is supposed to know something about the law and often does, though sometimes again he is an ignoramus. So, the governing *élite* contains individuals who wear labels appropriate to political offices of a certain altitude—ministers, Senators, Deputies, chief justices, generals, colonels, and so on—making the apposite exceptions for those who have found their way into that exalted company without possessing qualities corresponding to the labels they wear.

2036. Such exceptions are much more numerous than the exceptions among lawyers, physicians, engineers, millionaires (who have made their own money), artists of distinction, and so on; for the reason, among others, that in these latter departments of human activity the labels are won directly by each individual, whereas in the *élite* some of the labels—the label of wealth, for instance—are hereditary. . . . Wealth, family, or social connexions also help in many other cases to win the label of the *élite* in general, or of the governing *élite* in particular, for persons who otherwise hold no claim upon it.

2037. In societies where the social unit is the family the label worn by the head of the family also benefits all other members. In Rome, the man who became Emperor generally raised his freedmen to the higher class, and oftentimes, in fact, to the governing *élite*. . . . In our societies, the social unit is the individual; but the place that the individual occupies in society also benefits his wife, his children, his connexions, his friends.

2038. If all these deviations from type were of little importance, they might be disregarded, as they are virtually disregarded in cases where a diploma is required for the practice of a profession. Everyone knows that there are persons who do not deserve their diplomas, but experience shows that on the whole such exceptions may be overlooked.

2039. One might, further, from certain points of view at least, disregard deviations if they remained more or less constant quantitatively—if there were only a negligible variation in proportions between the total of a class and the people who wear its label without possessing the qualities corresponding.

2040. As a matter of fact, the real cases that we have to consider in our societies differ from those two. The deviations are not so few that they can be disregarded. Then again, their number is variable, and the variations give rise to situations having an important bearing on the social equilibrium. We are therefore required to make a special study of them.

2041. Furthermore, the manner in which the various groups in a population intermix has to be considered. In moving from one group to another an individual generally brings with him certain inclinations, sentiments, attitudes, that he has acquired in the group from which he comes, and that circumstance cannot be ignored.

2042. To this mixing, in the particular case in which only two groups, the élite and the non-élite, are envisaged, the term "circulation of élites" has been applied—in French, circulation des élites.

2043. In conclusion we must pay special attention (1), in the case of one single group, to the proportions between the total of the group and the number of individuals who are nominally members of it but do not possess the qualities requisite for effective membership; and then (2), in the case of various groups, to the ways in which transitions from one group to the other occur, and to the intensity of that movement—that is to say, to the velocity of the circulation.

2044. Velocity in circulation has to be considered not only absolutely but also in relation to the supply of and the demand for certain social elements. A country that is always at peace does not require many soldiers in its governing class, and the production of generals may be overexuberant as compared with the demand. But when a country is in a state of continuous warfare many soldiers are necessary, and though production remains at the same level it may not meet the demand. That, we might note in passing, has been one of the causes for the collapse of many aristocracies.

2045. Another example. In a country where there is little industry and little commerce, the supply of individuals possessing in high degree the qualities requisite for those types of activity exceeds the demand. Then industry and commerce develop and the supply, though remaining the same, no longer meets the demand.

2046. We must not confuse the state of law with the state of fact. The latter alone, or almost alone, has a bearing on the social equilibrium. There are many examples of castes that are legally closed, but into which, in point of fact, new-comers make their way, and often in large numbers. On the other hand, what difference does it make if a caste is legally open, but conditions de facto prevent new accessions to it? If a person who acquires wealth thereby becomes a member of the governing class, but no one gets rich, it is as if the class were closed; and if only a few get rich, it is as if the law erected serious barriers against access to the caste. Something of that sort was observable towards the end of the Roman Empire. People who acquired wealth entered the order of the curials. But only a few individuals made any money. Theoretically we might examine any number of groups. Practically we have to confine ourselves to the more important. We shall proceed by successive approximations, starting with the simple and going on to the complex.

2047. *Higher class and lower class in general.* The least we can do is to divide society into two strata: a higher stratum, which usually contains the rulers, and a lower stratum, which usually contains the ruled. . . . Above, in §§1723 f., we noted a varying distribution of residues in the various social groupings, and chiefly in the higher and the lower class. Such heterogeneousness is a fact perceived by the most superficial glance.

2048. Changes in Class I and Class II residues occurring within the two social strata have an important influence in determining the social equilibrium. They have been commonly observed by laymen under a special form, as changes in "religious" sentiments, so called, in the higher stratum of society. It has often been noted that there were times when religious sentiments seemed to lose ground, others when they seemed to gain in strength, and that such undulations corresponded to social movements of very considerable scope. The uniformity might be more exactly described by saying that in the higher stratum of society Class II residues gradually lose in strength, until now and again they are reinforced by tides upwelling from the lower stratum.

2049. Religious sentiments were very feeble in the higher classes in Rome towards the end of the Republic; but they gained notably in strength thereafter, through the rise to the higher classes of men from the lower, of foreigners that is, freedmen, and others, whom the Roman Empire raised in station. They gained still further in intensity in the days of the decadent Roman Empire, when the government passed into the hands of a military plebs and a bureaucracy originating in the lower classes. That was a time when a predominance of Class II residues made itself manifest in a decadence in literature and in the arts and sciences, and in invasions by Oriental religions and especially Christianity.

2050. The Protestant Reformation in the sixteenth century, the Puritan Revolution in Cromwell's day in England, the French Revolution of 1789, are examples of great religious tides originating in the lower classes and rising to engulf the sceptical higher classes. An instance in our day would be the United States of America, where this upward thrust of members of lower classes strong in Class II residues is very intense; and in that country one witnesses the rise of no end of strange and wholly unscientific religions—such as Christian Science—that are utterly at war with any sort of scientific thinking, and a mass of hypocritical laws for the enforcement of morality that are replicas of laws of the European Middle Ages.

2051. The upper stratum of society, the *élite*, nominally contains certain groups of peoples, not always very sharply defined, that are called aristocracies. There are cases in which the majority of individuals belonging to such aristocracies actually possess the qualities requisite for remaining there; and then again there are cases where considerable numbers of the individuals making up the class do not possess those requisites. Such people may occupy more or less important places in the governing *élite* or they may be barred from it.

2052. In the beginning, military, religious, and commercial aristocracies and plutocracies—with a few exceptions not worth considering—must have constituted parts of the governing *élite* and sometimes have made up the whole of it. The victorious warrior, the prosperous merchant, the opulent plutocrat, were men of such parts, each in his own field, as to be superior to the average individual. Under those circumstances the label corresponded to an actual capacity. But as time goes by, considerable, sometimes very considerable, differences arise between the capacity and the label; while on the other hand, certain aristocracies originally figuring prominently in the rising *élite* end by constituting an insignificant element in it. That has happened especially to military aristocracies.

2053. Aristocracies do not last. Whatever the causes, it is an incontestable fact that after a certain length of time they pass away. History is a graveyard of aristocracies. . . .

2054. They decay not in numbers only. They decay also in quality, in the sense that they lose their vigour, that there is a decline in the proportions of the residues which enabled them to win their power and hold it. The governing class is restored not only in numbers, but—and that is the more important thing—in quality, by families rising from the lower classes and bringing with them the vigour and the proportions of residues necessary for keeping themselves in power. It is also restored by the loss of its more degenerate members.

2055. If one of those movements comes to an end, or worse still, if they both come to an end, the governing class crashes to ruin and often sweeps the whole of a nation along with it. Potent cause of disturbance in the equilibrium is the accumulation of superior elements in the lower classes and, conversely, of inferior elements in the higher classes. . . .

2056. In virtue of class-circulation, the governing *élite* is always in a state of slow and continuous transformation. It flows on like a river, never being today what it was yesterday. From time to time sudden and violent disturbances occur. There is a flood—the river overflows its banks. Afterwards, the new governing *élite* again resumes its slow transformation. The flood has subsided, the river is again flowing normally in its wonted bed.

2057. Revolutions come about through accumulations in the higher strata of society—either because of a slowing-down in class-circulation, or from other causes—of decadent elements no longer possessing the residues suitable for keeping them in power, and shrinking from the use of force; while meantime in the lower strata of society elements of superior quality are coming to the fore, possessing residues suitable for exercising the functions of government and willing enough to use force.

2058. In general, in revolutions the members of the lower strata are captained by leaders from the higher strata, because the latter possess the intellectual qualities required for outlining a tactic, while lacking the combative residues supplied by the individuals from the lower strata.

2059. Violent movements take place by fits and starts, and effects therefore do not follow immediately on their causes. After a governing class, or a nation, has maintained itself for long periods of time on force and acquired great wealth, it may subsist for some time still without using force, buying off its adversaries and paying not only in gold, but also in terms of the dignity and respect that it had formerly enjoyed and which constitute, as it were, a capital. . . .

2060. *The elements.* The form of a society is determined by all the elements acting upon it and it, in turn, reacts upon them. We may therefore say that a reciprocal determination arises. Among such elements the following groups may be distinguished: 1. soil, climate, flora, fauna, geological, mineralogical, and other like conditions; 2. elements external to a given society at a given time, such as the influences of other societies upon it—external, therefore, in space; and the effects of the previous situation within it—external, therefore, in time; then 3: internal elements, chief among which, race, residues (or better, the sentiments manifested by them), proclivities, interests, aptitudes for thought and observation, state of knowledge, and so on. Derivations also are to be counted among these latter.

2061. These elements are not independent: for the most part, they are interdependent. Among them, moreover, are to be classed such forces as tend to prevent dissolution, ruin, in societies that endure. When, therefore, a society is organized under a certain form that is determined by the other elements, it acts in its turn upon them, and they, in that sense, are to be considered as in a state of interdependence with it. Something of the sort is observable in animal organisms. The form of the organs determines the kind of life the animal leads, but that manner of living in its turn has its influence upon the organs.

. . . . .

2063. An exhaustive study of social forms would have to consider at least the chief elements that determine them, disregarding those elements only which seem to be of secondary or incidental influence. But such a study is not at present possible, any more than an exhaustive study of plant or animal forms is possible, and we are therefore obliged to confine ourselves to a study covering a part only of the subject. Fortunately for our project, not a few of the elements have an influence upon human proclivities and sentiments, so that by taking account of residues we indirectly take account of them as well.

. . . . .

2066. But however many, however few, the elements that we choose to consider, we assume at any rate that they constitute a system, which we may call the "social system"; and the nature and properties of that system we propose to investigate. The system changes both in form and in character in course of time. When, therefore, we speak of "the social system" we mean that system taken both at a specified moment and in the successive transformations which it undergoes within a specified period of time. So when one speaks of the solar system, one means that system taken both at a specified moment and in the successive moments which go to make up a greater or lesser period of time.

2067. *The state of equilibrium.* If we intend to reason at all strictly, our first obligation is to fix upon the state in which we are choosing to consider the social system, which is constantly changing in form. The real state, be it static or dynamic, of the system is determined by its conditions. Let us imagine that some modification in its form is induced artificially. At once a reaction will take place, tending to restore the changing form to its original state as modified by normal change. If that were not the case, the form, with its normal changes, would not be determined but would be a mere matter of chance.

2068. We can take advantage of that peculiarity in the social system to define the state that we choose to consider and which for the moment we will indicate by the letter X. We can then say that the state X is such a state that if it is artificially subjected to some modification different from the modification it undergoes normally, a reaction at once takes place tending to restore it to its real, its normal, state. That gives us an exact definition of the state X.

2069. The state X is ever in process of change, and we are not able, nor do we care, to consider it that way in all its minute detail. . . . If we want to figure on the element of patriotism, we cannot follow each soldier in every move he makes from the day when he is called to arms to the day when he falls on a battle-field.

For our purposes it is enough to note the gross fact that so many
men have died for their country. Or again, the hand of a watch
moves and stops, stops and moves, yet in measuring time we disregard that circumstance and figure as though the movement of
the hand were continuous. Let us therefore consider successive states
X_1, X_2, X_3 . . . reached at certain intervals of time that we fix on
for the purpose of getting at the states which we choose to consider and which are such that each one of the elements that we
elect to consider has completed its action. To see the situation more
clearly, we might look at a few examples. Pure economics affords a
very simple one. Let us take a person who in a given unit of time—
every day, we will say—barters bread for wine. He begins with no
wine, and stops bartering when he has a certain quantity of wine.
In Figure 6, the axis of time is Ot, and ab, bc, cd, de . . . are spaces

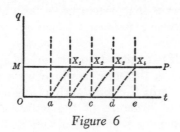

Figure 6

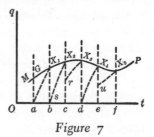

Figure 7

representing equal units of time. The axis of the quantities of wine
is Oq. At the beginning of the first unit of time, the individual has
no wine—his position is at a; at the end he has the quantity bX_1 of
wine—his position is at X_1. Exactly the same transaction is repeated
every day, and at the end of every day, or of every unit of time,
the individual's position is at X_1, X_2, X_3. . . . All those points fall
within a line, MP, parallel to Ot, and the distance between the two
lines is equal to the quantity of wine that the individual acquires
through exchange each day. The line MP is called the line of
equilibrium and, in general, is the line determined by the equations
of pure economics. It does not have to be a line parallel to the axis
Ot, for there is no reason why exactly the same transaction should
be repeated every day. It may, for example, be the line MP in Figure
7: ab, bc, cd . . . are still equal units of time, but at the begin-
nings of the various periods the individual's position is at a, s, r, d, u
. . . and at the ends at X_1, X_2, X_3, X_4, X_5. . . . The line $M\,X_1$,

X_2, X_3, X_4, X_5 . . . is still called the line of equilibrium. When it is said that pure economics gives the theory of the economic equilibrium, it means that pure economics shows how the final positions, X_1, X_2, X_3 . . . are reached from the points a, s, r, d, u . . . and nothing more. Now let us consider the more general case. In Figure 7, ab, bc, cd . . . are no longer equal to one another, but represent different periods of time, which we choose in order to examine a phenomenon at the end of each of them, the length of the period being determined by the time required for an element to complete the particular action that we have chosen to consider. The points a, s, r, d, u . . . represent the state of the individual at the beginning of the action; X_1, X_2, X_3 . . . the state of the individual when it is completed. The line $M X_1, X_2$ . . . P is the line of the state X.

2070. That definition is identical, barring the mere difference in form, with the one given in §2068. In fact, if we start in the first place with the definition just given of the state X_1, we see that the action of each element having been completed, society cannot of itself assume any form other than the form X_1, and that if it were made artificially to vary from that form, it should tend to resume it; for otherwise, its form would not be entirely determined, as was assumed, by the elements considered. In other words, if society has reached a point, X_1 (Figure 8), following such a path, aX_1, that at X_1 the action of the elements which we choose to consider is complete; and if society is artificially made to vary from X_1, the variation can be brought about only: (1) by forcing society to points such as l, n . . . which are located outside the line aX_1; or (2), by forcing it to a point m on the line aX_1. In the first case, society should tend to return to X_1; otherwise its state would not be completely determined, as was assumed, by the elements considered. In the second case, the hypothesis would be in contradiction with our assumption that the action of the elements is complete; for it is complete only at X_1, and is incomplete at m; at the latter point the elements considered are still in action and they carry society from m to X_1.

Using the definition we gave in §2068 as the point of departure, we see, conversely, that if after society has been artificially made to vary from the point X_1, it tends to return to X_1, the phenomenon indicates one of two things: either, as in the first case above, that society has been brought to the points l, n . . . which are different from the points determined by the elements considered, or that society has been brought to a point *m*, at which the action of the elements considered is incomplete. If instead of reaching the points X_1, X_2, X_3 . . . successively the system were to traverse the line X_1, X_2, X_3 in a continuous movement, there would be nothing to change in the definitions just given. One would need merely to say that if the system were made artificially to deviate from the line X_1, X_2 . . . it would tend at once to return to it; and that if the effect of the elements is to impel the system along that line, their action would not be complete unless the system were located on that line, and on no other.

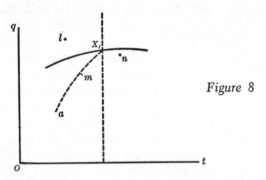

Figure 8

2071. So we get the precise and rigorous definition that we said we were intending to give of the state we are about to consider. To become more familiar with it let us now look at some analogies, much as one looks at a sphere to get some conception of the shape of the Earth.

For a concrete example, the state X is analogous to the state of a river, and the states X_1, and X_2 . . . to the states of the same river taken day by day. The river is not motionless; it is flowing, and the slightest modification we try to effect in its form and in the manner of its flow is the cause of a reaction that tends to reproduce the original state.

2072. For an abstract case . . . the state X that we are considering is analogous to the state of dynamic equilibrium in a physical system, the states X_1, X_2 . . . to successive positions of equilibrium in that system. The state X, one might also add, is analogous to the state of equilibrium in a living organism.

.   .   .   .   .

2074. There is another analogy that we cannot disregard if we would go somewhat deeply into this matter. The state X is analogous to the state called a *statistic* equilibrium in the kinetic theory of gases. To make that clearer, suppose we consider a particular case, the consumption, for instance, of cigars of a given quality within a given territory. The states X_1, X_2, X_3 . . . represent, hypothetically, the annual consumptions of such cigars. Let us begin by assuming that they are all more or less equal. Then we would say that the consumption of cigars is constant. By that we do not mean that every individual smokes the same number of cigars each year. We know very well that such numbers vary widely. But the variations more or less offset one another, so that the resultant is zero or, to be more exact, approximately zero. To be sure, it may happen that so many of these variations will be in the same direction that the resultant will no longer be approximately zero, but such a probability is so slight that we need not consider it; and that is what we mean when we say that the consumption is constant. If, instead, the probability is not so slight, fluctuations around the constant total of consumption will be observable, such fluctuations following the law of probabilities. But suppose X_1, X_2, X_3 . . . represent increasing consumptions. We can then repeat, with the proper modifications, everything we have just said. We are in no sense assuming that the individual consumptions are on the increase. We know they are extremely variable. We are speaking of a *statistic* equilibrium, where variations offset one another in such a way that the resultant is an increasing total consumption. And such increasing total consumption may have a probability so great as to eliminate fluctuations depending on probabilities; or a probability not so great, and then fluctuations will occur. So, in preparing ourselves by studying particular cases of that sort we find it easy to grasp the general significance of X_1, X_2, X_3 . . . for consumptions varying in any manner whatsoever.

2075. Extend to an entire social system what we have seen to hold for a system of consumers of one brand of cigars, and the result will be a clear conception of the analogy we have in view for the states X_1, X_2, X_3. . . .

2076. We could continue to designate the social states that we elect to consider with the letters X, and X_1, X_2 . . . , but that manner of designating things soon begins to weary and one would prefer to have them given names. We could choose a name at random, but it is perhaps better to borrow it from something more or less like the thing we intend to designate by it. So, stopping at the mechanical analogy, we will call the states X and X_1, X_2 . . . *states of equilibrium.* But the meaning of the term as we use it has to be sought strictly within the definitions that we gave in §§2068–69, (due attention being paid to the argument in §2074.)

2077. We have now simplified our problem by deciding to consider certain successive states instead of the numberless imperceptible mutations that lead up to them. We now have to go on along that path and try to reduce the problem of mutual correlations and the number of elements that we are to consider to greater simplicity.

. . . . .

2079. *Organization of the social system.* The economic system is made up of certain molecules set in motion by tastes and subject to ties (checks) in the form of obstacles to the acquisition of economic values. The social system is much more complicated, and even if we try to simplify it as far as we possibly can without falling into serious errors, we at least have to think of it as made up of certain molecules harbouring residues, derivations, interests, and proclivities, and which perform, subject to numerous ties, logical and non-logical actions. In the economic system the non-logical element is relegated entirely to tastes and disregarded, since tastes are taken as data of fact. One might wonder whether the same thing might not be done for the social system, whether we might not relegate the non-logical element to the residues, then take the residues as data of fact and proceed to examine the logical conduct that originates in the residues. That, indeed, would yield a science similar to pure, or even to applied, economics. But unfortunately the similarity ceases when we come to the question of correspondences with reality. The hypothesis that in satisfying their tastes human beings perform economic actions which may on the whole be considered logical is not too far removed from realities, and the inferences from those hypotheses yield a general form of the economic phenomenon in which divergences from reality are few and not very great, save in certain cases (most important among them the matter of savings). Far removed from realities, instead, is the hypothesis that human beings draw logical inferences from residues and then proceed to act accordingly. In activity based on residues human beings use derivations more frequently than strictly logical reasonings, and therefore to try to predict their conduct by considering their manners of reasoning would be to lose all contacts with the real. Residues are not, like tastes, merely sources of conduct; they function throughout the whole course of the conduct developing from the source, a fact that becomes apparent in the substitution of derivations for logical reasonings. A science, therefore, based on the hypothesis that logical inferences are drawn from certain given residues would yield a general form of the social phenomenon having little or no contact with reality—it would be a sociology more or less like a non-Euclidean geometry or the geometry of a four-dimensional space. If we would keep within realities, we have to ask experience to acquaint us not only with certain fundamental residues, but with the various ways in which they function in determining the conduct of human beings.

2080. Let us consider the molecules of the social system, in other words, individuals, who are possessed of certain sentiments manifested by residues. . . . We may say that present in individuals are mixtures of groups of residues that are analogous to the mixtures of chemical compounds found in nature, the groups of residues themselves being analogous to the chemical compounds. We have . . . examined the character of such mixtures and groups, and we found that while some of them appear to be virtually independent, others also are correlated in such a manner that an accentuation in the one is offset by an attenuation in others, and vice versa. Such mixtures and groups, whether dependent or independent, are now to be considered among the elements determining the social equilibrium.

2081. Residues manifest themselves through derivations. These are indications of the forces operating upon the social molecules.

. . . . .

2083. In this matter of derivations, the capital fact is that they do not correspond exactly to the residues in which they originate. In that lie the chief obstacles to the constitution of a social science; for derivations only are known to us, and we are sometimes at a loss as to how to find our way back from the derivations to the residues that underlie them. . . . Derivations, furthermore, contain many principles that are not explicitly stated, which are taken for granted, and as a result they are gravely lacking in definiteness. . . . To remedy that difficulty, we have to collect large numbers of derivations associated with one same subject-matter, and then find in them a constant element that can be distinguished from variable elements.

2084. Even when there is some rough correspondence between

derivation and residue, the derivation usually oversteps the terms of the residue and oversteps reality. It indicates an extreme limit of which the residue falls short, and very very often contains an imaginary element that states a goal far beyond the goal which would be set if it expressed the residue exactly. If, furthermore, the imaginary element expands and evolves, the results are myths, religions, ethical systems, theologies, systems of metaphysics, ideals. That happens more especially when the sentiments corresponding to derivations are intense, and the more readily, the greater the intensity.

. . . . .

2086. In trying to get back from derivations to residues, it must not be overlooked that a given residue, B, may have any number of derivations, T, T', T'' . . . that are readily interchangeable. So: 1. If T appears in one society and T' in another, one cannot conclude that the two societies have different corresponding residues: they may have the same residue, B. 2. To replace T' with T is of little or no avail as regards modifying social forms, since the substitution has no effect on the residue B, which plays a much more important part than the derivations in determining those forms. 3. But the fact that the subject of the conduct considers or does not consider the substitution a matter of indifference may have its effect, not through that opinion as such, but through the sentiments that it manifests. 4. The derivations T, T', T'' . . . may show reciprocal contradictions. If two logico-experimental propositions were contradictory they would destroy each other. Two contradictory derivations not only may subsist simultaneously but may even reinforce each other. Sometimes other derivations are brought in to eliminate the contradiction and establish harmony, but that is of quite secondary importance. . . .

2087. *Composition of residues and derivations.* We have so far been considering separate groups of residues. Now let us see how they work when they are taken together. The situation in one of its aspects bears some analogy to the compounding of chemical elements, and under another aspect, to the composition of forces in mechanics. Speaking in general terms, suppose a society is being influenced by certain sentiments corresponding to the residue groups A, B, C . . . manifested through the derivations a, b, c. . . . Now let us give each of those groups of residues a quantitative index corresponding to the intensity of its action as a group. So we get the indices a, β, γ. . . . Let us further designate as S, T, U . . . the derivations, myths, theories, and so forth, that correspond to the residue groups, A, B, C. . . . The social system will then be in equilibrium under the action of the forces a, β, γ . . . which are exerted approximately in the direction indicated by the derivations S, T, U . . . due account being taken of counter-forces. In that we are merely restating what we have just said in a new form.

2088. Keeping to this new form we get the following propositions: 1. One cannot, as is usually done, estimate the effects of each group of residues, or variations in the intensity of the group, taking the group all by itself. If the intensity varies in one group, variations, generally, must occur in other groups if the equilibrium is to be maintained. That is a different sort of dependence from the one mentioned in §2080. Different things have to be designated by different names. Suppose, then, we use the term *dependence, first type* for the direct dependence between various groups of residues, and the term *dependence, second type* for the indirect dependence arising from the proviso that the equilibrium has to be maintained, or from some other requirement of the kind. 2. The real movement takes place according to the resultant of the forces a, β, γ . . . and in no way corresponds to the imaginary resultant—if there be such a thing—of the derivations S, T, U. . . . 3. The derivations show only the direction in which certain movements are tending to evolve (§2087); but that direction is not, generally speaking, the direction that would be indicated by the derivation taken in its strict literalness, as would be the case with a logico-experimental proposition. We have frequently seen that two contradictory derivations can hold side by side, a thing that would be impossible in the case of two logical propositions. The two propositions $A = B$ and $B < > A$ are logically contradictory and so cannot both be true. But as derivations they can get along together perfectly well and mean one and the same thing, namely, that the A's are trying to rule the B's, using the first proposition to weaken the resistance of people who, though not partisans of the B's, would not like to see them reduced to subjection; and using the second proposition to inspire those who are already partisans of the A's to action. 4. Ordinarily, if the social system does not move in the direction indicated by the residues, A, to which the force a corresponds, the reason is not that there has been direct resistance to A, and much less that the derivation S corresponding to A has been refuted; but that the movement in accord

with *A* has been deflected under the influence of the residues *B, C.*
. . . It is important to distinguish, among these latter, the residues
belonging to various classes; for owing to the tendency of the class
as a whole to remain virtually constant, one should be on watch
for the action rather of the various classes than of each single
residue.

2089. Better to picture the difference between interdependences
of the first and the second types, one might consider a given society.
Its existence is in itself a fact, and then we have the various facts
that are taking place within it. If we look at the first fact and these
latter facts simultaneously, we will say that they are all interdependent. If we separate them, we will say that the latter facts are all
mutually dependent (dependence, first type) and are furthermore
interdependent through the first fact (dependence, second type).
We can also say that the fact of the existence of society results from
the facts observable within it, that, in other words, these latter facts
determine the social equilibrium; and, further again, that if the fact
of the existence of a society is given, the facts arising within it are
no longer altogether arbitrary but must satisfy a certain condition,
namely, that the equilibrium being given, the facts which determine
it cannot be altogether arbitrary.

Let us look at [an illustration] of the difference between interdependences of the first and second types. The inclination of the
Romans towards formalism in practical life tended to produce, maintain, and intensify formalism in religion, law, and politics; and
vice versa. That would be an interdependence of the first type. But
we get an interdependence of the second type in the fact that the
inclination of the Romans to independence managed to survive owing to the fact that political formalism averted the dangers of anarchy. That was what actually happened down to the last years of
the Republic. The inclination of the Romans to political formalism
weakening about that time (chiefly because the old Romans had
given way to people of other stocks), their inclination to independence was also weakened, and they were obliged to accept imperial despotism as a lesser evil. Had it not given ground in that
way, Roman society would have broken down either through internal revolutions or through foreign conquest, exactly as happened,
and for identical reasons, with Poland. In this case there is no direct
interdependence between Class II residues (inclination to formalism) and Class V residues (inclination to independence)—which

would be a dependence of the first type. There is an indirect interdependence, arising from the fact that for the Roman community at that time and under those circumstances, the position in which the index of the inclination to independence (residues of personal integrity) remained constant while the index of political formalism (residues of group-persistence) fell off, was not a position of equilibrium (interdependence, second type).

2090. From the manner of operation of interdependences of the second type it is evident that their effects oftentimes become much less promptly manifest than the effects of interdependences of the first type—for a change in the equilibrium must first have occurred and then have had its repercussions on other residues. For the same reasons, interdependences of the second type will play a more important rôle than those of the first type in the rhythmical character of social movements.

. . . . .

2105. *Properties of the social system.* A system of material atoms and molecules has certain thermic, electrical, and other properties. So a system made up of social molecules also has certain properties that it is important to consider. One among them has been perceived, be it in a rough and crude fashion, in every period of history—the one to which with little or no exactness the term "utility," or "prosperity," or some other such term, has been applied. We must now dig down into the facts to see whether something definite can be found underlying these vague expressions, and its character determined.

. . . . .

2110. To get a more exact picture, one has to state just what norms—they have to be to some extent arbitrary—one intends to follow in determining the entities that one is trying to define. Pure economics has succeeded in doing that. It has taken a single norm, the individual's satisfaction, and it has further set down that of that satisfaction he is the only judge. So economic "utility" or "ophelimity" came to be defined. But if we set ourselves the problem, after all so simple, of ascertaining quite apart from the individual's judgment just what is most advantageous to him, it soon appears that we require a norm, and that it has to be arbitrary. Shall we say, for instance, that it will be to his advantage to suffer physically for the sake of a moral satisfaction, or shall we say the opposite? Shall we say that it is better for him to seek wealth exclusively, or to apply himself to something else? In pure economics we left the decision to him. If now we are going to deprive him of that function, we must find someone else to whom it can be assigned.

2111. *Utility.* Whoever the judge we choose, whatever the norms we decide to follow, the entities so determined have certain common properties, and we shall now look at them. Once we have fixed upon the norms we elect to follow in determining a certain state as the limit that an individual or a community is assumed to approach, and once we have given numerical indices to the different states that more or less approximate the limit state, so that the state closest to it has an index larger than the index of the state farthest removed, we can say that those indices are indices of a state X. Then, as usual, for the purpose of avoiding the inconvenience of using mere letters of the alphabet as terms, we will substitute some name or other for the letter X, taking the name, again as usual, in order to avoid a jargon too baroque, from something of kindred nature. When we know, or think we know, just what thing is advantageous to an individual or a community, we say that it is "beneficial" for both individuals and communities to exert themselves to obtain it, and judge the utility they enjoy the greater, the nearer they come to obtaining it. By simple analogy, therefore, and for no other reason, we shall apply the term "utility" to the entity X just described.

. . . . .

2115. The important thing, first of all, is to distinguish cases according as we are thinking of the individual, the family, a community, a nation, the human race. And not only are the utilities of those various entities to be considered; a further distinction has to be drawn between their direct utilities and the utilities that they derive indirectly through their mutual relationships. So, disregarding other distinctions that it might be of advantage to make, and keeping to such as are absolutely indepensable, we find ourselves obliged to deal with the following varieties:

a. *Utility to the Individual:*
  a-1. Direct
  a-2. Indirect, resulting from the fact that the individual is part of a community
  a-3. Utility to an individual, as related to the utilities to others
b. *Utility to a Given Community*
  b-1. Direct utility to communities, considered apart from other communities

b-2. Indirect utility, arising by reaction from other communities
b-3. Utility to one community as related to the utilities to other communities

Far from coinciding, these various utilities oftentimes stand in overt opposition. . . .

2116. Without departing from the logico-experimental domain, further distinctions may be drawn and the different utilities considered in two ways: as one of the members of the community pictures them to himself, and as an outside views them, or a member of the community trying as far as he can to render an objective judgment. An individual who has a vivid sense of the direct utility, *a*-1, and little or no sense of the indirect, *a*-2, will simply look to his own convenience and not concern himself with his fellow-citizens; whereas a person judging that individual's conduct objectively will see that he is sacrificing the community to his own advantage.

2117. Nor have we yet done with our distinctions. Each of the varieties indicated may be considered with reference to time—in reference to the present, that is, and to one point or another in the future; nor will the conflicts between those various utilities be found any less sharp than between the others, nor can there be less difference as regards the person who judges them under sway of sentiment and the person who views them objectively.

. . . . .

2120. *Net utility.* Taking account of the three types of utility noted in the case of a single individual, we get as a result the net utility that the individual enjoys. He may, on the one hand, suffer a direct damage and on the other hand, as a member of a community, secure an indirect advantage; and the latter may be so great as more than to offset the direct damage, so that in the end there is a certain gain for a remainder. So for a group. If we could get indices for these various utilities, and take their sum, we would have the total or net utility of the individual or group.

2121. *Maximum utility* OF *an individual or group.* Since the utility just mentioned has an index, it may, possibly, in a certain state have a larger index than in a state more or less close to it—that is to say, it may have a maximum. . . .

2122. When we consider a definite species of utility with reference to an individual, we get indices of partial utilities and also an index of the total net utility; and that is what makes it possible to estimate the utility which the individual enjoys under given circumstances.

Furthermore, if, as circumstances vary, the index of his net utility, which began by increasing, ends by decreasing, there will be a certain point at which it reaches a maximum. All the problems that we stated previously in qualitative terms then become quantitative and involve problems of maxima. Instead of asking whether an individual achieves his own happiness through observing certain norms, we ask whether and to what extent his ophelimity increases, and once on that road, we end by asking how and when such ophelimity attains its maximum.

                                 . . . . .

2125. Difficult as these problems may be practically, they are theoretically easier than others on which we must now touch.

2126. So far we have considered the maxima of utility of an individual and of a community taken apart from other individuals and communities. Still left is the problem of those same maxima when individuals or communities are taken relatively to one another. For the sake of brevity we shall speak only of individuals in what follows, but the reasoning will apply just as well to comparisons of distinct communities. If the utilities of single individuals were homogeneous quantities and could therefore be compared and reduced to a sum, our study would not, theoretically at least, be difficult. We would simply take the sum of the utilities of the various individuals and so get the utility of the community they constitute —and that would be taking us back to problems already examined.

2127. But the business is not so simple. The utilities of various individuals are heterogeneous quantities, and a sum of such quantities is a thing that has no meaning; there is no such sum, and none such can be considered. If we would have a sum that stands in some relation to the utilities of the various individuals, we must first find a way to reduce those utilities to homogeneous quantities that can be summed.

2128. *Maximum of ophelimity* FOR *a community in political economy.* A problem of just that character arose in economics and had to be solved by that science. It will be well to consider it briefly, that we may be the better prepared to solve the more difficult sociological problem. In economics the equilibrium can be determined provided we stipulate that every individual achieves the maximum of ophelimity. The ties can be posited in such a way that the equilibrium will be perfectly determined. If, now, certain ties are suppressed, the perfect determination will come to an end, and the equilibrium will be possible at an infinite number of points at which maxima of individual ophelimities are attained. In the first case, only movements leading to the determined point of equilibrium were possible; in the second, other movements also are possible. These are of two quite distinct types. Movements of a first type, P, are such that, beneficial to certain individuals, they are necessarily harmful to others. Movements of a second type, Q, are such that they are to the advantage, or to the detriment, of all individuals without exception. The points P are determined by equating with zero a certain sum of homogeneous quantities dependent on heterogenous ophelimities.

2129. Consideration of the two types of points, P and Q, is of great importance in political economy. When the community stands at a point, Q, that it can leave with resulting benefits to all individuals, procuring greater enjoyments for all of them, it is obvious that from the economic standpoint it is advisable not to stop at that point, but to move on from it as far as the movement away from it is advantageous to all. When, then, the point P, where that is no longer possible, is reached, it is necessary, as regards the advisability of stopping there or going on, to resort to other considerations foreign to economics—to decide on grounds of ethics, social utility, or something else, which individuals it is advisable to benefit, which to sacrifice. From the strictly economic standpoint, as soon as the community has reached a point P it has to stop. That point therefore plays in the situation a rôle analogous to the rôle of the point where the maximum of individual ophelimity is attained and at which, accordingly, the individual stops. Because of that analogy it has been called *point of maximum ophelimity* FOR *the community.* . . .

2130. If a community could be taken as a single individual, it would have a maximum of ophelimity just as a single individual has; there would, that is, be points at which the ophelimity of the community would attain a maximum. These points would not be the same as the points Q indicated in §2128. Since, in fact, advances from those points can be made with resulting benefit to all the individuals in a community, it is obvious that the ophelimity of the community might be increased in that fashion. But it cannot be said that such points would coincide with the points P. Let us take a community made up of just two persons, A and B. We can move from a point P, adding 5 to A's ophelimity and taking 2 from the ophelimity of B, and so reaching a point s; or adding 2 to A's ophelimity and taking 1 from B's, so that a point t is reached. We cannot know at which of the two points, s, t, the ophelimity of the community will be greater or less until we know just how the ophelimities of A and of B are to be compared; and precisely because they cannot be compared, since they are heterogeneous quantities, no maximum ophelimity of the community exists; whereas a maximum ophelimity for the community can exist, since it is determined independently of any comparison between the ophelimities of different individuals.

2131. *The maximum of utility* FOR *a community, in sociology.* Now let us take all that over into sociology. In so far as he acts logically, every individual tries to secure a maximum of individual utility, as explained in §2122. If we assume that some of the ties imposed by public authority are suppressed without being replaced by others, an infinite number of positions of equilibrium with the provisos of individual maxima as indicated become possible. Public authority interposes to require some and prohibit others. Let us assume that it acts logically and with the sole purpose of achieving a certain utility. (That rarely is the case; but that fact we need not consider here, since we are envisaging not a real, concrete situation, but a theoretical, hypothetical one.) In such a case the government must necessarily compare—we need not now ask with reference to what criteria—the various utilities. When it shuts a thief up in prison, it compares the pain that it inflicts upon him with the utility resulting from it to honest people, and it roughly guesses that the latter at least offsets the former; otherwise it would let the thief go. For the sake of brevity we have here compared two utilities only. A government of course—as best it can, and that is often badly enough—compares all the utilities it is aware of. Substantially, it does at a guess what pure economics does with scientific exactness: it makes certain heterogeneous quantities homogeneous by giving them certain coefficients, thence proceeding to add the resulting quantities and so determine points of the type P.

. . . . .

2133. In pure economics a community cannot be regarded as a person. In sociology it can be considered, if not as a person, at least as a unit. There is no such thing as the ophelimity of a community; but a community utility can roughly be assumed. So in pure economics there is no danger of mistaking the maximum of ophelimity *for* a community for a non-existent maximum of ophelimity *of* a community. In sociology, instead, we must stand watchfully on guard against confusing the maximum of utility *for* a community with the maximum of utility *of* a community, since they both are there.

2134. Take, for instance, the matter of population increase. If we think of the utility *of* the community as regards prestige and military power, we will find it advisable to increase population to the fairly high limit beyond which the nation would be impoverished and its stock decay. But if we think of the maximum of utility *for* the community, we find a limit that is much lower. Then we have to see in what proportions the various social classes profit by the increase in prestige and military power, and in what different proportion they pay for it with their particular sacrifices. When proletarians say that they refuse to have children because children merely increase the power and profits of the ruling classes, they are dealing with a problem of maximum utility *for* the community. . . .

. . . . .

2170. *The use of force in society.* Societies in general subsist because alive and vigorous in the majority of their constituent members are sentiments corresponding to residues of sociality (Class IV). But there are also individuals in human societies in whom some at least of those sentiments are weak or indeed actually missing. That fact has two interesting consequences which stand in apparent contradition, one of them threatening the dissolution of a society, the other making for its progress in civilization. What at bottom is there is continuous movement, but it is a movement that may progress in almost any direction.

2171. It is evident that if the requirement of uniformity (residues IV-β) were so strongly active in all individuals in a given society as to prevent even one of them from breaking away in any particular from the uniformities prevalent in it, such a society would have no internal causes for dissolution; but neither would it have any causes for change, whether in the direction of an increase, or of a decrease, in the utility of the individuals or of the society. On the other hand if the requirement of uniformity were to fail, society would not hold together, and each individual would go his own way. . . . Societies that endure and change are therefore situated in some intermediate condition between those two extremes.

. . . . .

2173. For the reader who has followed us thus far it is needless to add that, in view of the effects of this greater or lesser potency of the sentiments of uniformity, one may foresee out of hand that two theologies will put in an appearance, one of which will glorify the immobility of one or another uniformity, real or imaginary, the other of which will glorify movement, progress, in one direction or another. That is what has actually happened in history. There have been popular Olympuses where the gods fixed and determined once and for all how human society was to be. . . . On the other hand, from the days of ancient Athens down to our own, the lord gods of Movement in a Certain Direction have listened to the prayers of their faithful and now sit triumphant in our latter-day Olympus, where Progress Optimus Maximus reigns in sovereign majesty. So that intermediate situation of society has usually been attained as the resultant of many forces, prominent among them the two categories mentioned, which envisage different imaginary goals and correspond to different classes of residues.

2174. To ask whether or not force ought to be used in a society, whether the use of force is or is not beneficial, is to ask a question that has no meaning; for force is used by those who wish to preserve certain uniformities and by those who wish to overstep them; and the violence of the ones stands in contrast and in conflict with the violence of the others. . . .

2175. Nor is there any particular meaning in the question as to whether the use of violence to enforce existing uniformities is beneficial to society, or whether it is beneficial to use force in order to overstep them; for the various uniformities have to be distinguished to see which of them are beneficial and which deleterious to society. Nor, indeed, is that enough; for it is further necessary to determine whether the utility of the uniformity is great enough to offset the harm that will be done by using violence to enforce it, or whether detriment from the uniformity is great enough to overbalance the damage that will be caused by the use of force in subverting it; in which detriment and damage we must not forget to reckon the very serious drawback involved in the anarchy that results from any frequent use of violence to abolish existing uniformities, just as among the benefits and utilities of maintaining frankly injurious uniformities must be counted the strength and stability they lend to the social order. So, to solve the problem as to the use of force, it is not enough to solve the other problem as to the utility, in general, of certain types of social organization; it is essential also and chiefly to compute all the advantages and all the drawbacks, direct and indirect. Such a course leads to the solution of a scientific problem; but it may not be and oftentimes is not the course that leads to an increase in social utility. It is better, therefore, if it be followed only by people who are called upon to solve a scientific problem or, to some limited extent, by certain individuals belonging to the ruling class; whereas social utility is oftentimes best served if the members of the subject class, whose function it is not to lead but to act, accept one of the two theologies according to the case—either the theology that enjoins preservation of existing uniformities, or the theology that counsels change.

2176. What we have just said serves to explain, along with the theoretical difficulties, how it comes about that the solutions that are usually found for the general problem have so little and sometimes no bearing on realities. Solutions of particular problems come closer to the mark because, situate as they are in specific places and times, they present fewer theoretical difficulties; and because practical empiricism implicitly takes account of many circumstances that theory, until it has been carried to a state of high perfection, cannot explicitly appraise.

Considering violations of material conformities among modern civilized peoples, we see that, in general, the use of violence in repressing them is the more readily condoned in proportion as the violation can be regarded as an individual anomaly designed to attain some individual advantage, and the less readily condoned in proportion as the violation appears as a collective act aiming at some collective advantage, and especially if its apparent design be to replace general norms prevailing with certain other general norms.

2177. That states all that there is in common between the large numbers of facts in which a distinction is drawn between so-called private and so-called political crimes. A distinction, and often a very sharp distinction, is drawn between the individual who kills or steals for his own benefit and the individual who commits murder or theft with the intent of benefiting a party. In general, civilized countries grant extradition for the former, but refuse it for the latter. In the same way one notes a continually increasing leniency towards crimes committed during labour strikes or in the course of other economic, social, or political struggles. There is a more and more conspicuous tendency to meet such aggressions with merely passive resistance, the police power being required not to use arms, or else permitted to do so only in cases of extreme necessity. . . . Punishment by judicial process is also becoming less and less vigorous. Criminals are either not convicted or, being convicted, are released in virtue of some probation law, failing of which, they can still rely on commutations, individual pardons, or general amnesties, so that, sum total, they have little or nothing to fear from the courts. In a word, in a vague, cloudy, confused sort of way, the notion is coming to the fore that an existing government may make some slight use of force against its enemies, but no great amount of force, and that it is under all circumstances to be condemned if it carries the use of force so far as to cause the death of considerable numbers, of a small number, a single one, of its enemies; nor can it rid itself of them, either, by putting them in prison or otherwise.

2178. What now are the correlations that subsist between this method of applying force and other social facts? We note, as usual, a sequence of actions and reactions, in which the use of force appears now as cause, now as effect. As regards the governing class, one gets, in the main, five groups of facts to consider: 1. A mere handful of citizens, so long as they are willing to use violence, can force their will upon public officials who are not inclined to meet violence with equal violence. If the reluctance of the officials to resort to force is primarily motivated by humanitarian sentiments, that result ensues very readily; but if they refrain from violence because they deem it wiser to use some other means, the effect is often the following: 2. To prevent or resist violence, the governing class resorts to "diplomacy," fraud, corruption—governmental authority passes, in a word, from the lions to the foxes. The governing class bows its head under the threat of violence, but it surrenders only in appearances, trying to turn the flank of the obstacle it cannot demolish in frontal attack. In the long run that sort of procedure comes to exercise a far-reaching influence on the selection of the governing class, which is now recruited only from the foxes, while the lions are blackballed. The individual who best knows the arts of sapping the strength of the foes of "graft" and of winning back by fraud and deceit what seemed to have been surrendered under pressure of force, is now leader of leaders. The man who has bursts of rebellion, and does not know how to crook his spine at the proper times and places, is the worst of leaders, and his presence is tolerated among them only if other distinguished endowments offset that defect. 3. So it comes about that the residues of the combination-instinct (Class I) are intensified in the governing class, and the residues of group-persistence (Class II) debilitated; for the combination-residues supply, precisely, the artistry and resourcefulness required for evolving ingenious expedients as substitutes for open resistance, while the residues of group-persistence stimulate open resistance, since a strong sentiment of group-persistence cures the spine of all tendencies to curvature. 4. Policies of the governing class are not planned too far ahead in time. Predominance of the combination instincts and enfeeblement of the sentiments of group-persistence result in making the governing class more satisfied with the present and less thoughtful of the future. The individual comes to prevail, and by far, over family, community, nation. Material interests and interests of the present or a near future come to prevail over the ideal interests of community or nation and interests of the distant future. The impulse is to enjoy the present without too much thought for the morrow. 5. Some of these phenomena become observable in international relations as well. Wars become essentially economic. Efforts are made to avoid conflicts with the powerful and the sword is rattled only before the weak. Wars are regarded more than anything else as speculations. A country is often unwittingly edged towards war by nursings of economic conflicts which, it is expected, will never get out of control and turn into armed conflicts. Not seldom, however, a war will be forced upon a country by peoples who are not so far advanced in the evolution that leads to the predominance of Class I residues.

2179. As regards the subject class, we get the following relations, which correspond in part to the preceding: 1. When the subject class contains a number of individuals disposed to use force and with capable leaders to guide them, the governing class is, in many cases, overthrown and another takes its place. That is easily the case where governing classes are inspired by humanitarian sentiments primarily, and very very easily if they do not find ways to assimilate the exceptional individuals who come to the front in the subject classes. A humanitarian aristocracy that is closed or stiffly exclusive represents the maximum of insecurity. 2. It is far more difficult to overthrow a governing class that is adept in the shrewd use of chicanery, fraud, corruption; and in the highest degree difficult to overthrow such a class when it successfully assimilates most of the individuals in the subject class who show those same talents, are adept in those same arts, and might therefore become the leaders of such plebeians as are disposed to use violence. Thus left without leadership, without talent, disorganized, the subject class is almost always powerless to set up any lasting régime. 3. So the combination-residues (Class I) become to some extent enfeebled in the subject class. But that phenomenon is in no way comparable to the corresponding reinforcement of those same residues in the governing class; for the governing class, being composed, as it is, of a much smaller number of individuals, changes considerably in character from the addition to it or withdrawal from it of relatively small numbers of individuals; whereas shifts of identical numbers produce but slight effects in the enormously greater total of the subject class. For that matter the subject class is still left with many individuals possessed of combination-instincts that are applied not to politics or activities connected with politics but to arts and trades independent of politics. That circumstance lends stability to societies, for the governing class is required to absorb only a small number of new individuals in order to keep the subject class deprived of leadership. However, in the long run the differences in temperament between the governing class and the subject class become gradually accentuated, the combination-instincts tending to predominate in the ruling class, and instincts of group-persistence in the subject class. When that difference becomes sufficiently great, revolution occurs. 4. Revolution often transfers power to a new governing class, which exhibits a reinforcement in its instincts of group-persistence and so adds to its designs of present enjoyment aspirations towards ideal enjoyments presumably attainable at some future time—scepticism in part gives way to faith. 5. These considerations must to some extent be applied to international relations. If the combination-instincts are reinforced in a given country beyond a certain limit, as compared with the instincts of group-persistence, that country may be easily vanquished in war by another country in which that change in relative proportions has not occurred. The potency of an ideal as a pilot to victory is observable in both civil and international strife. People who lose the habit of applying force, who acquire the habit of considering policy from a commercial standpoint and of judging it only in terms of profit and loss, can readily be induced to purchase peace; and it may well be that such a transaction taken by itself is a good one, for war might have cost more money than the price of peace. Yet experience shows that in the long run, and taken in connexion with the things that inevitably go with it, such practice leads a country to ruin. The combination-instincts rarely come to prevail in the whole of a population. More commonly that situation arises in the upper strata of society, there being few if any traces of it in the lower and more populous classes. So when a war breaks out one gazes in amazement on the energies that are suddenly manifested by the masses at large, something that could in no way have been foreseen by studying the upper classes only. Sometimes, as happened in the case of Carthage, the burst of energy may not be sufficient to save a country, because a war may have been inadequately prepared for and be incompetently led by the ruling classes, and soundly prepared for and wisely led by the ruling classes of the enemy country. Then again, as happened in the wars of the French Revolution, the energy in the masses may be great enough to save a country because, though the war may have been badly prepared for by its ruling classes, preparations and leadership have been even worse in the ruling classes of the enemy countries, a circumstance that gives the constituent members of the lower strata of society time to drive their ruling class from power and replace it with another of greater energy and possessing the instincts of group-persistence in greater abundance. Still again, as happened in Germany after the disaster at Jena, the energy of the masses may spread to the higher classes and spur them to an activity that proves most effective as combining able leadership with enthusiastic faith.

2180. These, then, are the main, the outstanding phenomena, but other phenomena of secondary or incidental importance also figure. Notable among such is the fact that if a ruling class is unable or unwilling or incompetent to use force to eradicate violations of uniformities in private life, anarchic action on the part of the subject class tends to make up for the deficiency. . . . Whenever the influence of public authority declines, little states grow up within the state, little societies within society. So, whenever judicial process fails, private or group justice replaces it, and vice versa.

2190. Suppose a certain country has a governing class, A, that assimilates the best elements, as regards intelligence, in the whole population. In that case the subject class, B, is largely stripped of such elements and can have little or no hope of ever overcoming the class A so long as it is a battle of wits. If intelligence were to be combined with force, the dominion of the A's would be perpetual, for as Dante says, *Inferno*, xxxi, vv. 55–57 (Fletcher translation):

For if the machination of the mind
To evil-will be added and to might,
Of no defence is competent mankind.

But such a happy combination occurs only for a few individuals. In the majority of cases people who rely on their wits are or become less fitted to use violence, and *vice versa*. So concentration in the class A of the individuals most adept at chicanery leads to a concentration in class B of the individuals most adept at violence; and if that process is long continued, the equilibrium tends to become unstable, because the A's are long in cunning but short in the courage to use force and in the force itself; whereas the B's have the force and the courage to use it, but are short in the skill required for exploiting those advantages. But if they chance to find leaders who have the skill—and history shows that such leadership is usually supplied by dissatisfied A's—they have all they need for driving the A's from power. Of just that development history affords countless examples from remotest times all the way down to the present.

2191. . . . If one judges superficially, one may be tempted to dwell more especially on the slaughter and pillaging that attend a revolution, without thinking to ask whether such things may not be manifestations—as regrettable as one may wish—of sentiments, of social forces, that are very salutary. If one should say that, far from being reprehensible, the slaughter and robbery are signs that those who were called upon to commit them deserved power for the good of society, he would be stating a paradox, for there is no relationship of cause and effect, nor any close and indispensable correlation, between such outrages and social utility; but the paradox would still contain its modicum of truth, in that the slaughter and rapine are external symptoms indicating the advent of strong and courageous people to places formerly held by weaklings and cowards. In all that we have been describing in the abstract many revolutions that have actually occurred in the concrete, from the revolution which gave imperial rule to Augustus down to the French Revolution of '89. If the class governing in France had had the faith that counsels use of force and the will to use force, it would never have been overthrown and, procuring its own advantage, would have procured the advantage of France. Since it failed in that function, it was salutary that its rule should give way to rule by others; and since, again, it was the resort to force that was wanting, it was in keeping with very general uniformities that there should be a swing to another extreme where force was used even more than was required. . . .

[When] a governing class divests itself too completely of the sentiments of group-persistence, it easily reaches a point where it is unfit to defend, let alone its own power, what is far worse, the independence of its country. In such a case, if the independence is to be deemed an advantage, it must also be deemed an advantage to be rid of a class that has become incompetent to perform the functions of defence. As a rule it is from the subject class that individuals come with the faith and the resolve to use force and save a country.

. . . .

2203. *Cycles of interdependence.* Let us go back and think once more of the elements upon which the social equilibrium depends; and since, unfortunately, we cannot consider them all and take their interdependences into account in all strictness, suppose we . . . consider a restricted group of elements, to be selected, naturally, from among the more important, gradually enlarging the groups thereafter so as to have them include as many elements as possible. As for the interdependences, we will use method 2a instead of method 2b, as indicated in §1732. . . .

2204. An element of a given group acts upon elements in other groups, either apart from the other elements in its own group or in conjunction with them. Suppose we call the effect it has when considered apart from the other elements in its group the *direct* effect; the effect it has in virtue of its combination with other elements in its group, the *indirect* effect. In so doing we shall be continuing the analysis we began in §2089. There we divided facts into two categories: 1. The fact of the existence of a society. 2. The facts observable in that society, in other words, the elements from which the fact of its existence results. Let us now first divide this second category into groups, and then go on to select one element from each group and try to determine the effect that it has, as a distinct unit, upon the elements in other groups (*direct* effect) as well as the effect it has upon them when it is considered as operating in conjunction with the other elements in its own group (*indirect* effect).

2205. And now let us turn to the matter of interdependence among the groups. To be as brief as possible, suppose we indicate the following elements by letters of the alphabet: Residues, a; interests, b; derivations, c; social heterogeneity and circulation, d. . . .

2206. We may say, accordingly: (I) That a acts upon b, c, d; (II) that b acts upon a, c, d; (III) that c acts upon a, b, d; (IV) that d acts upon a, b, c.

From what we have been saying . . . it is evident that Combination I yields a very considerable portion of the social phenomenon; and those writers who have regarded ethics as the foundation of society may have had a remote and inadequate perception of that fact. In it also lies the modicum of truth that is to be found in metaphysical doctrines which make facts dependent upon "concepts," since "concepts" reflect, though very confusedly, residues and sentiments corresponding to residues. It is Combination I also that assures continuity in the history of human societies, since the category a varies slightly or slowly.

Combination II also yields a very considerable portion of the social phenomenon, and it too varies but slightly and slowly and contributes to the continuity of human societies. The importance of Combination II was noticed by the followers of "economic determinism"; but they fell into the error of substituting the part for the whole and disregarding the other combinations. Combination III is the least important of all. Failure to perceive that fact has rendered the lucubrations of humanitarians, "intellectuals," and worshippers of the goddess Reason, erroneous, inconclusive, fatuous. However, to a greater degree than any of the others it is known to us through literature, and a far greater importance is commonly attached to it than it really has in society. Combination IV is of no mean importance, a fact remarked of old by Plato and Aristotle, to say nothing of other ancient writers. . . .

2207. It must not be forgotten that actions and reactions follow one on another indefinitely and, as it were, in a circle: that is to say, beginning with Combination I one goes on to Combination IV and from IV back again to I. In Combination I the element a was acting upon d; in IV the element d is acting upon a; then one goes back again to Combination I, so that a is again acting upon d, and so on. In virtue, therefore, of Combination I a variation in a causes variations in the other elements, b, c, d; and just to make the situation more manageable in language, we will give the variations in a, b, c, d that are effected in virtue of Combination I the name of *immediate effects*. But in virtue of the other combinations, variations in b, c, d also effect variations in a; and because of the circular movement this variation reacts upon Combination I and gives rise to new variations in a, b, c, d. To these variations we will, again for mere purposes of convenience, give the name of *mediate effects*. Sometimes it is necessary to consider two or more combinations simultaneously. . . . The state of concrete equilibrum observable in a given society is a resultant of all these effects, of all these actions and reactions. It is therefore different from a state of theoretical equilibrium obtained by considering one or more of the elements a, b, c, d instead of considering all. Political economy, for instance, deals with category b, and one of its branches is pure economics. Pure economics yields a theoretical equilibrium that is different, still within category b, from another theoretical equilibrium yielded by applied economics; and different from other theoretical equilibria that could be obtained by combining b with some of the elements a, c, d; and different, again, from the theoretical equilibrium that most nearly approximates the concrete and is obtained by combining all the elements a, b, c, d.

2208. This will all be clearer if we give a less abstract form to what we have just been saying, and at the same time proceed from particular cases to more general ones, following the inductive method. Suppose we locate the protection of industries by import duties in the group b. We first get its economic effects, direct and indirect; and these are the concern primarily of economics, which is the science of the group b. We shall not go into them here, but merely note certain effects that we find it necessary to consider for our purposes. Among these we shall have to consider economic effects that have so far been more or less neglected by the science of economics. As a rule, champions of free trade have considered low prices, implicitly at least, as an advantage to a population at large, whereas champions of protection have regarded low prices as an evil. The first view is readily acceptable to anyone thinking chiefly of consumption, the latter to anyone thinking chiefly of production. From the scientific standpoint they are both of little or no value, since they are based on an incomplete analysis of the situation. A forward step along the scientific path was taken when the theories of mathematical economics supplied a proof that, in general, the direct effect of protection is a destruction of wealth. If one were free to go on and add an axiom, which is implicitly taken for granted by many economists, that any destruction of wealth is an "evil," one could logically conclude that protection is an "evil." But before such a proposition can be granted the indirect economic effects and the social effects of protection have to be known. Keeping to the former for the moment, we find that protection transfers a certain amount of wealth from a part, A, of the population to a part B, through the destruction of a certain amount of wealth, q, the amount representing the costs of the operation. If, as a result of this new distribution of wealth, the production of wealth does not increase by a quantity greater than q, the operation is economically detrimental to a population as a whole; if it increases by a quantity greater than q, the operation is economically beneficial. The latter case is not to be barred a priori; for the element A contains the indolent, the lazy, and people, in general, who make little use of economic combinations; whereas the element B comprises the people who are economically wide-awake and are always ready for energetic enterprise—people who know how to make effective use of economic combinations. Going on, then, to consider in general not only economic but social effects, one has to distinguish between dynamic effects, which ensue for a brief period of time after protection has been established, and static effects, which ensue after protection has been established for a certain length of time. A distinction must further be drawn between the effects on productions that are readily susceptible of increase, such as manufactures in general, and the effects on productions not so susceptible of increase, such as the agricultural. The dynamic effect is more considerable in the case of the manufacturer than in the case of the farmer. When protection is established those manufacturers who already own factories for protected goods, and persons who are shrewd enough to anticipate protection or to go out and get it, enjoy temporary monopolies, and these come to an end only when new manufacturers enter the field to compete with established firms—that takes time, and often not a short time. Farmers, on the other hand, have little to fear from new enterprise, and for them, therefore, the dynamic effect is not so very different from the static. Furthermore, protection may encourage new industries and so increase, if not the profits, at least the numbers, of manufacturers. That may also happen in agriculture, though on a very much smaller scale, and the ordinary effect of agricultural protection is merely to replace one kind of acreage with another. The static effect, on the other hand, is less considerable on the profits of manufacturers than on the profit of the farmer. It increases the earnings of the farmer, while competition cuts down the earnings of the manufacturer from his temporary monopoly. For that very reason industrial protection usually destroys more wealth than agricultural protection, for with the latter the new earnings, which represent a mere transfer of wealth, are saved from destruction.

2209. Let us look at the *immediate* effects on the other groups.

Combination II. The most perceptible effects are on *d*, that is to say, on social heterogenousness. The dynamic effects of industrial protection enrich not only individuals who are endowed with technical talents, but especially individuals who have talents for financial combinations or gifts for manipulating the politicians who confer the benefits of protection. Some individuals possess such endowments in conspicuous degree. They grow rich and influential, and come to "run the country." The same is true of politicians who are clever at selling the benefits of protection. All such persons possess Class I residues in high intensities, and Class II residues in fairly low intensities. On the other hand, people in whom endowments of character are more notable than technical or financial talents, or who lack the gift for clever political manoeuvring, are pushed down the ladder. Deriving no benefit from protection, they are the ones who pay its costs. The static effects are not identical—they are analogous in that, though they enrich far fewer persons, they nevertheless open new fields for the activities of individuals who have endowments of talent and cunning, and they increase the industrial population, often at the expense of the agricultural. In short, to put the situation briefly, when account is taken, in making up the governing class, of the imaginary examinations that we used for illustration in §2027, the higher grades have to be given to individuals in whom Class I residues are numerous and intense and who know how to use them in garnering the fruits of protection; and the lower grades, to individuals in whom Class I residues are few and feeble, or, if they are numerous and strong, are not skilfully exploited. So it results that industrial protection tends to strengthen Class I residues in the governing class. Class-circulation, furthermore, is accelerated. In a country where there is little industry an individual born with a good assortment of combination-instincts finds far fewer opportunities for using them than an individual born in a country where there are many industries and where new enterprises are starting every day. The very art of manipulating protectionist favours offers a wide field of activity for people whose talents lie in that direction, even though they do not use them

directly in industry. Carrying on the analogy suggested, one may
say that the examinations for purposes of discovering the candidate
best equipped with Class I residues are held more frequently and
attract larger numbers of aspirants.

2210. No very appreciable effects are apparent on residues, a,
if only for the reason that residues change but slowly. On the
other hand, effects upon derivations, c, are very considerable, and
one notes a rank florescence of economic theories in defence of
protection, many of which are comparable to the dedications and
sonnet sequences that were addressed to wealthy feudal lords in a
day gone by as bids for pensions.

2211. *Combination III.* Derivations act feebly, or not at all,
upon residues, a, feebly upon interests, b, a little more potently upon
social heterogeneity, d, for in any society persons who have the knack
for praising people in power find ready admission to the governing
class. Schmoller might never have been named to the Prussian House
of Lords had he been a free-trader; on the other hand English
free-traders win favours from a so-called "Liberal" government.
That gives us an indirect effect outside our categories: the interests,
b, acting upon derivations, c, and they in turn upon social heterogeneity, d.

2212. *Combination IV.* Here again we get effects of great importance, not so much in the influence of heterogeneity upon residues—in view, as usual, of their relative stability—as in the influence
of interests.

. . . . .

2215. . . . After interests have, thanks to protection, brought into
the governing class individuals richly endowed with Class I residues,
those individuals in their turn influence interests and stimulate the
whole country in the direction of economic pursuits and industrial-
ism. The thing is so noticeable that it has not escaped even casual
observers, or people who wear the blinders of mistaken theories, and
it has often been described as an "increase in capitalism" in modern
societies. Then going on, arguing as usual *post hoc, propter hoc,*
the "increase in capitalism" has been taken as the cause of a decline
in moral sentiments (group-persistence).

2216. That, really, is a case of an indirect, a mediate, effect: interests, in other words, have influenced heterogeneity; the latter, in
its turn, now reacts upon interests; and through a sequence of actions
and reactions, an equilibrium is established in which economic pro-

duction and class-circulation become more intense, and the composition of the governing class is profoundly modified.

2217. The increase in economic production may be great enough to exceed the destruction of wealth caused by protection; so that, sum total, protection may yield a profit and not a loss in wealth; it may therefore prove (though not necessarily so) that the economic prosperity of a country has been enhanced by industrial protection.

2218. That, notice, is a *mediate* effect, coming about through the influence of industrial protection upon social heterogeneity and class-circulation, which go on in turn to react upon the economic situation. It is possible for that reason to suppress the first link in the chain; and so long as the second is kept, the effect will follow just the same. For that reason, again, if protection were to act in a different wise upon social heterogeneity and class-circulation, the effect also would be different; and that is what actually happens, as a rule, with agricultural protection. Halting, therefore, at the point in the cycle where we now stand, we may say that it will be possible to get the indirect, the *mediate*, effect of an increase in economic prosperity either through industrial protection or through a free trade that removes a burdensome agricultural protection. . . .

. . . . .

2220. It must not be forgotten that so far we have been very roughly sketching a first picture of the situation. A great deal still remains to be done in filling in the secondary details. This is not just the place to do that; but we are obliged to eliminate one other imperfection in it that is due to our stopping at a certain point in the cycle, whereas actually we have to go on and look at further mediate effects that are quite different.

2221. If no counter-forces stood in the way, and the cycle of actions and reactions were to go on indefinitely, economic protection and its effects ought to go on becoming progressively greater; and that is what is actually observable in many countries during the nineteenth century. But as a matter of fact counter-forces do develop, and increasingly so. Speaking now not of the particular case of protection, but in general, such forces may be noted in the modifications that the *élite* undergoes, and in variations in the circumstances that make the cyclical movement possible. History shows that when the proportions between Class I and Class II residues in the *élite* begin to vary, the movement does not continue indefinitely in one direction, but is sooner or later replaced by a movement in a counter-direction. Such counter-movements often result from wars, as was the case in the conquest of Greece by Rome, Greece at the time possessing Class I residues in very great abundance, while in Rome the advantage lay with the residues of group-persistence (Class II). Then again, the counter-movement to a movement that has been in progress for a fairly long time has resulted from internal revolutions, a striking case being the change from the Republic to the Empire in Rome, which was primarily a social revolution and profoundly altered proportions of residues in the ruling class. Considering the two processes together we may say, in general and roughly, that when the counter-movement does not come from wars, it comes from revolutions, much as when the fruit is ripe on the tree either it is plucked by a human hand or it falls naturally to the ground, but in either event is removed from the tree. The cause just mentioned—modifications in the *élite*—is among the major ones determining the undulating form that the movement assumes. . . .

. . . . .

2230. [*Speculators and rentiers.*]   In §§2026 f. we suggested a general classification of social strata and in §2052 we alluded to the relations of that classification to the classification of aristocracies. That is not all there is to the matter. It may properly be the subject of many other considerations, one among which is of the first importance.

2231. It is of an economic character. Writers have confused and persist in confusing under the term "capitalists" (1) owners of savings and persons who live on interest from property and (2) promoters of enterprise—"*entrepreneurs*." That confusion is a great hindrance to an understanding of the economic phenomenon and an even greater hindrance to an understanding of human society. In reality those two sorts of "capitalists" often have interests that are different. Sometimes indeed they are diametrically opposed and stand in even greater conflict than the interests of the classes known as "capitalist" and "proletarian."

. . . . .

2233. . . . . Suppose we put in one category, which we may call S, individuals whose incomes are essentially variable and depend upon the person's wide-awakeness in discovering sources of gain. In that group, generally speaking and disregarding exceptions, will be found . . . promoters   of   enterprise . . . *entrepreneurs* . . . and   with them will be stockholders in industrial and commercial corporations (but not bondholders, who will more fittingly be placed in our group next following). Then will come owners of real estate in cities where building speculation is rife; and also landowners—on a similar condition that there be speculation in the lands about them; and then stock-exchange speculators and bankers who make money on governmental, industrial, and commercial loans. We might further add all persons depending upon such people—lawyers, engineers, politicians, working-people, clerks—and deriving advantage from their operations. In a word, we are putting together all persons who directly or indirectly speculate and in one way or another manage to increase their incomes by ingeniously taking advantage of circumstances.

2234. And let us put into another category, which we may call R, persons who have fixed or virtually fixed incomes not depending to any great extent on ingenious combinations that may be conceived by an active mind. In this category, roughly, will be found persons who have savings and have deposited them in savings-banks or invested them in life-annuities; then people living on incomes from government bonds, certificates of the funded debt, corporation bonds, or other securities with fixed interest-rates; then owners of real estate and lands in places where there is no speculation; then farmers, working-people, clerks, depending upon such persons and in no way depending upon speculators. In a word, we so group together here all persons who neither directly nor indirectly depend on speculation and who have incomes that are fixed, or virtually fixed, or at least are but slightly variable.

2235. Just to be rid of the inconvenience of using mere letters of the alphabet, suppose we use the term "speculators" for members of category S and the French term *rentiers* for members of category R. . . . In the speculator group Class I residues predominate, in the *rentier* group, Class II residues. That that should be the case is readily understandable. A person of pronounced capacity for economic combinations is not satisfied with a fixed income, often a very small one. He wants to earn more, and if he finds a favourable opportunity, he moves into the S category. The two groups perform functions of differing utility in society. The S group is primarily responsible for change, for economic and social progress. The R group, instead, is a powerful element in stability, and in many cases counteracts the dangers attending the adventurous capers of the S's. A society in which R's almost exclusively predominate remains stationary and, as it were, crystallized. A society in which S's predominate lacks stability, lives in a state of shaky equilibrium that may be upset by a slight accident from within or from without.

. . . . .

[2313. *Rentiers*] are, in general, secretive, cautious, timid souls, mistrustful of all adventure, not only of dangerous ventures but of such as have any remotest semblance of not being altogether safe. They are very readily managed and even robbed by anyone deft in the opportune use of sentiments corresponding to Class II residues, which are very strong in the R's. Speculators, on the other hand, are usually expansive personalities, ready to take up with anything new, eager for economic activity. They rejoice in dangerous economic ventures and are on the watch for them. In appearance they are always submissive to the man who shows himself the stronger; but they work underground and know how to win and hold the substance of power, leaving the outward forms to others. No rebuff discourages them. Chased away in one direction, they come buzzing back, like flies, from some other. If the sky darkens, they take to their cellars, but out they come the moment the tornado has blown over. With their unfaltering perseverance and their subtle art of combinations they override all obstacles. Their opinions are always the opinions most useful to them at the moment. Conservatives yesterday, they are Liberals today, and they will be Anarchists tomorrow, if the Anarchists show any signs of getting closer to power. But the speculators are shrewd enough not to be all of one colour, for it is better to have friends in all parties of any importance. On the stage one may see them battling one another, Catholics and pro-Semites, monarchists and republicans, free-traders and Socialists. But behind the scenes they join hands, speculators all, and march in common accord upon any enterprise that is likely to mean money. When one of them falls, his enemies treat him mercifully, in the expectation that if occasion requires they too will be shown mercy. Neither the R's nor the S's are very adept in the use of force, and both are afraid of it. The people who use force and are not afraid of it make up a third group, which finds it very easy to rob the R's, rather more difficult to rob the S's; for if the S's are defeated and overthrown today, they are back on their feet and again in power tomorrow.

. . . . .

2235 [*continued*]. Members of the R group must not be mistaken for "conservatives," nor members of the S group for "progressives," innovators, revolutionaries. They may have points in common with such, but there is no identity. There are evolutions, revolutions, innovations, that the R's support, especially movements tending to restore to the ruling classes certain residues of group-persistence that had been banished by the S's. A revolution may be made against the S's —a revolution of that type founded the Roman Empire, and such, to some extent, was the revolution known as the Protestant Reformation. Then too, for the very reason that sentiments of group-persistence are dominant in them, the R's may be be so blinded by sentiment as to act against their own interests. They readily allow themselves to be duped by anyone who takes them on the side of sentiment, and time and time again they have been the artisans of their own ruin. If the old feudal lords, who were endowed with R traits in a very conspicuous degree, had not allowed themselves to be swept off their feet by a sum of sentiments in which religious enthusiasm was only one element, they would have seen at once that the Crusades were to be their ruin. . . .

Nor are the categories R and S to be confused with groupings that might be made according to economic occupation. There again we find points of contact, but not full coincidence. A retail merchant often belongs to the R group, and a wholesale merchant too, but the wholesaler will more likely belong to the S group. Sometimes one same enterprise may change in character. An individual of the S type founds an industry as a result of fortunate speculations. When it yields or seems to be yielding a good return, he changes it into a corporation, retires from business, and passes over into the R group. A large number of stockholders in the new concern are also R's—the ones who bought stock when they thought they were buying a sure thing. If they are not mistaken, the business changes in character, moving over from the S type to the R type. But in many cases the best speculation the founder ever made was in changing his business to a corporation. It is soon in jeopardy, with the R's standing in line to pay for the broken crockery. There is no better business in this world than the business of fleecing the lambs—of exploiting the inexperience, the ingenuousness, the passions, of the R's. In our societies the fortunes of many many wealthy individuals have no other foundations.

2236. The differing relative proportions in which S types and R types are combined in the governing class correspond to differing types of civilization; and such proportions are among the principal traits that have to be considered in social heterogeneity. Going back, for instance, to the protectionist cycle examined above ($\S\S$2209 f.), we may say that in modern democratic countries industrial protection increases the proportion of S's in the governing class. That increase in turn serves to intensify protection, and the process would go on indefinitely if counter-forces did not come into play to check it. . . .

2237. *Government and its forms.* Among the complex phenomena that are observable in a society, of very great importance is the system of government. That is closely bound up with the character of the governing class, and both stand in a relationship of interdependence with all other social phenomena.

2238. Oftentimes, as usual, too much importance has been attached to forms at the expense, somewhat, of substance; and the thing chiefly considered has been the form that the political régime assumed. . . .

2239. Those who attach supreme significance to forms of government find it very important to answer the question, "What is the best form of government?" But that question has little or no meaning unless the society to which the government is to be applied is specified and unless some explanation is given of the term "best," which alludes in a very indefinite way to the various individual and social utilities. Although that has now and then been sensed, consideration of governmental forms has given rise to countless derivations leading up to this or that political myth, both derivations and myths being worth exactly zero from the logico-experimental standpoint, but both of them—or, rather the sentiments that they manifest—having, it may be, effects of great consequence in the way of influencing human conduct. It cannot be doubted that the sentiments manifested by the monarchical, republican, oligarchic, democratic, and still other faiths, have played and continue to play no mean part in social phenomena, as is the case with the sentiments underlying other religions. The "divine rights" of the prince, of the aristocracy, of the people, the proletariat, the majority—or any other divine right that might be imagined—have not the slightest experimental validity. We must therefore consider them extrinsically only, as facts, as manifestations of sentiments, operating, like other traits in the human beings that go to make up a given society, to determine its mode of being, its form. To say that no one of these "rights" has any experimental foundation does not, of course, in any way impugn the utility to society with which it may be credited. Such an inference would be justified if the statement were a derivation, since in such reasonings it is generally taken for granted that anything that is not rational is harmful. But the question of utility is left untouched when the statement is rigorously logico-experimental, since then it contains no such implicit premise.

2240. Here, as in dealing with other subjects of the kind, we stumble at the very first step on difficulties of terminology. That is natural enough: the objective investigations that we are trying to make require an objective terminology, whereas the subjective discussions that are commonly conducted can get along with the subjective terminology of ordinary parlance. Everyone recognizes that in our day "democracy" is tending to become the political system of all civilized peoples. But what is the exact meaning of the term "democracy"? It is even more vague than that vaguest of terms, "religion." We must therefore leave it to one side and turn to the facts that it covers.

2241. One observes at the outset a pronounced tendency on the part of modern civilized peoples to use a form of government where legislative power rests largely with an assembly elected by a part at least of the citizens. One further notes a tendency to augment that power and increase the number of citizens electing the assembly.

. . . . .

2244. We need not linger on the fiction of "popular representation"—poppycock grinds no flour. Let us go on and see what substance underlies the various forms of power in the governing classes. Ignoring exceptions, which are few in number and of short duration, one finds everywhere a governing class of relatively few individuals that keeps itself in power partly by force and partly by the consent of the subject class, which is much more populous. The differences lie principally, as regards substance, in the relative proportions of force and consent; and as regards forms, in the manners in which the force is used and the consent obtained.

2245. As we have elsewhere observed (§§2170 f.), if the consent were unanimous there would be no need to use force; but that extreme is unknown to fact. Another extreme has a few concrete illustrations—the case where a despot keeps himself in power by armed force against a hostile population (such cases all belong to the past); and then the case where a foreign power holds a reluctant people in subjection—of that there are still quite a few examples in the present. The reason why the equilibrium is much more unstable in the first case than in the other has to be sought in the prevalence of differing residues. The residues working in the satellites of the despot are not essentially different from those working in the despot's subjects, so that there is no faith available to inspire, and at the same time to restrain, the use of force; and as was the case with the praetorians, the janissaries, and the Mamelukes, satellites are readily tempted to make capricious use of their power, or else to abandon defence of the despot against the people. The ruling nation, on the other hand, generally differs in usages and customs, and sometimes in language and religion, from the subject nation. There is a difference in residues, therefore, and so plenty of faith to inspire use of force. But there may be plenty of faith in the subject nation to inspire resistance to oppression; and that is how, in the long run, the equilibrium may chance to be upset.

2246. It is in fear of that very outcome that conquering peoples try to assimilate their subject peoples, and when that can be done, it is by all odds the best way for them to assure their dominion. They often fail because they try to change residues by violence instead of taking advantage of existing residues. Rome had the faculty for this latter in pre-eminent degree, and so was able to assimilate the many peoples about her in Latium, Italy, and the Mediterranean basin.

2247. We have had incidental occasion already to remark that the policies of governments are the more effective, the more adept they are at utilizing existing residues, the less effective, the less skilful, and in general total failures when they set out to change residues by force; and to tell the truth, almost all explanations as to the success or failure of certain policies of this or that government come down in the end to that principle.

. . . . .

2249. To utilize the sentiments prevalent in a society for attaining a given purpose in in itself neither beneficial nor detrimental to society. The utility, or the detriment, depends upon the result achieved. If the result is beneficial, one gets a utility; if harmful, a detriment. Nor can it be said that when a governing class works for a result that will be advantageous to itself regardless of whether it will be beneficial, or the reverse, to its subject class, the latter is necessarily harmed. Countless the cases where a governing class working for its own exclusive advantage has further promoted the welfare of a subject class. In a word, utilization of the residues prevailing in a society is just a means, and its value the value of the results achieved.

. . . . .

2251. Consent and force appear in all the course of history as instruments of governing. They come forward in the legendary days of the *Iliad* and *Odyssey* to make the power of the Greek kings secure. They are discernible in the legends of the Roman kings. Later on, in historical times, in Rome they are busy under both Republic and Empire; and it is by no means to be taken for granted that the government of Augustus enjoyed any less support in the subject class than the various governments the last years of the Republic managed to secure. And so coming on through the Barbarian kings and the mediaeval republics down to the divine-right potentates of two or three centuries ago, and finally to our modern democratic régimes, we find all along the same mixture of force and consent.

2252. Just as derivations are much more variable than the residues that underlie them, so the forms in which force and consent express themselves are much more variable than the sentiments and interests in which they originate; and the differences in the relative proportions of force and consent are in large part due to varying relative proportions of sentiments and interests. The parallel between derivations and forms of government goes farther still. They both have less influence upon the social equilibrium than do the sentiments and interests that underlie them. . . .

2253. A governing class is present everywhere, even where there is a despot, but the forms under which it appears are widely variable. In absolute governments a sovereign occupies the stage alone. In so-called democratic governments it is the parliament. But behind the scenes in both cases there are always people who play a very important rôle in actual government. To be sure they must now and again bend the knee to the whims of ignorant and domineering sovereigns or parliaments, but they are soon back at their tenacious, patient, never-ending work, which is of much the greater consequence. In the Roman *Digesta* one may read truly splendid constitutions bearing the names of very wretched Emperors, just as in our day we have very fair legal codes that have been enacted by fairly brainless parliaments. The cause in both cases is the same: The sovereign leaves everything to his legal advisers, in some cases not even divining what they are having him do—and parliaments today even less than many a shrewd leader or king. And least of all King Demos! And such blindness on his part has at times helped to effect betterments in conditions of living in the face of his prejudices, not to mention much-needed steps in behalf of national defence. King Demos, good soul, thinks he is following his own devices. In reality he is following the lead of his rulers. But that very very often turns out to the advantage of his rulers only, for they, from the days of Aristotle down to our own, have made lavish use of the arts of bamboozling King Demos. Our plutocrats, like those of the late Roman Republic, are at all times busy making money, either on their own account or to sate the hungry maws of their partisans and accomplices; and for anything else they care little or nothing. Among the derivations which they use to show that their rule is to the advantage of a country, interesting is the assertion that the public is better qualified to pass on general questions than on special ones. The fact, in reality, is the precise opposite. One has to talk only for a very brief time with an uneducated person to see that he grasps special questions, which are usually concrete, much more clearly than general questions, which as a rule are abstract. But abstract questions have the advantage for people in power that whatever the answers that are given them by the public, they will be able to draw any inference they choose from them. The people sends to parliament men who are pledged to abolish interest on capital and "surplus value" in industry, and check the "greed" of the "speculators" (general questions); and those representatives now directly, now indirectly by helping others, increase the public debt beyond all bounds and consequently the interest paid to capital, maintain and in fact increase the "surplus value" enjoyed by manufacturers (many of whom fatten on political demagoguery), and put the government of the nation into the hands of speculators such as Volpi, who concluded the Peace of Lausanne, or of cabinet ministers such as Caillaux and Lloyd George.

2254. The governing class is not a homogeneous body. It too has a government—a smaller, choicer class (or else a leader, or a committee) that effectively and practically exercises control. Sometimes that fact is visible to the eye, as in the case of the Ephors of Sparta, the Council of Ten in Venice, the favourite ministers of absolute sovereigns, or the "bosses" in parliaments. A other times it is more or less hidden from view, as in the "caucus" in England, the political convention in the United States, the cliques of "speculator" chieftains who function in France and Italy, and so on. The tendency to personify abstractions or merely to think of them as objective realities inclines many people to picture the governing class as a person, or at least as a concrete unit, and imagine that it knows what it wants and executes by logical procedures designs which it had conceived in advance. . . . Ruling classes, like other social groups, perform both logical and non-logical actions, and the chief element in what happens is in fact the order, or system, not the conscious will of individuals, who indeed may in certain cases be carried by the system to points where they would never have gone of deliberate choice. In speaking of "speculators," we must not think of them as actors in a melodrama who administer and rule the world, executing wicked designs by stratagem dark. Such a conception of them would be no more real than a fairy-story. Speculators are just people who keep their minds on their business, and being well supplied with Class I residues, take advantage of them to make money, following lines of least resistance, as after all everybody else does. They hold no meetings where they congregate to plot common designs, nor have they any other devices for reaching a common accord. That accord comes about automatically; for if in a given set of circumstances there is one line of procedure where the advantage is greatest and the resistance least, the majority of those who are looking for it will find it, and though each of them will be following it on his own account, it will seem, without being so, that they are all acting in common accord. But at other times they will be carried along by the sheer force of the system to which they belong, involuntarily, and indeed against their wills, following the course that is required of the system. Fifty years ago "speculators" had no conception whatever of the state of affairs that prevails today and to which their activities have brought them. The road they have followed has been the resultant of an infinitude of minor acts, each determined by the present advantage. As is the case with all social phenomena, it has been the resultant of certain forces operating in conjunction with certain ties and in the face of certain obstacles. When we say that at the present time our speculators are laying the foundations for a war by continually increasing public expenditures, we in no sense mean that they are doing that deliberately—quite to the contrary! They are continually increasing public expenditures and fanning economic conflicts not in order to bring on a war, but in order

to make a direct profit in each little case. But that cause, though
an important one, is not the main cause. There is another of greater
importance—their appeal to sentiments of patriotism in the masses
at large, as a device for governing. Furthermore, the speculators in
the various countries are in competition with each other and are
using armaments to exact concessions from rivals. Other similar
causes are operating, and they all are leading to increases in armaments without that's being in any sense the consequence of precon-
ceived design. Not only that. Those men who are rich in Class I
residues sense intuitively, without needing to reason or theorize,
that if a great and terrible war should occur, one of its possible consequences might be that they would have to give way to men who
are rich in Class II residues. To such a war they are opposed in virtue of the same instinct that prompts the stag to run from the lion,
though they are glad to take on little colonial wars, which they can
superintend without any danger to themselves. It is on such interests and sentiments, not on any deliberate, premeditated resolve, that
their activities depend, and these accordingly may eventually carry
them to some objective that they may be aiming at, but also quite
as readily to points where they would never have dreamed of going. . . .

In dealing with speculators, as with other elements in the social
order, the ethical aspect and the aspect of social utility have to be
kept sharply distinguished. The speculators are not to be condemned
from the standpoint of social utility because they do things that are
censured by one or another of the current ethical systems; nor are
they to be absolved from any given ethical standpoint because they
have proved socially beneficial. The utility depends upon the circumstances in which the activities of the speculators are carried on,
and specifically upon the relative proportions of speculators to persons strong in Class II residues, either in the population at large
or in the governing classes. To determine and appraise such utility
is a quantitative, not a qualitative, problem. In our day, for instance,
the enormous development of economic production, the spread of
civilization to new countries, the remarkable rise in standards of living among all civilized peoples, are in large part the work of speculators. But they have been able to do that work because they came
from populations in which Class II residues were numerous and
strong: and it is doubtful, indeed it is hardly probable, that benefits
such as these could be realized if there were any great decline in

the Class II residues in our masses at large or even merely in our governing classes.

. . . . .

2274. . . . I. *Governments relying chiefly on physical force and on religious or other similar sentiments.* Examples would be the governments of the Greek cities in the age of the "tyrants," of Sparta, of Rome under Augustus and Tiberius, of the Venetian Republic during the last centuries of its existence, of many European countries in the eighteenth century. They show a governing class made up of individuals with Class II residues predominating over Class I residues. Class-circulation is generally slow. They are not expensive governments. On the other hand they fail to stimulate economic production, whether because they are conservative by temperament, recoiling from new enterprise, or because they put no premiums in class-circulation on individuals distinguished by instincts for economic combinations. If, however, such instincts survive in the population at large, the country may enjoy a moderate economic prosperity (Rome in the days of the High Empire) provided the government sets no obstacles in the way. But in the long run the obstacle usually arises, because the ideal of governments of that type is a nation that is crystallized in its institutions (Sparta, Rome in the day of the Low Empire, Venice of the Decadence). They may grow wealthy through conquests (Sparta, Rome); but since no new wealth is produced in that manner, the prosperity is necessarily precarious (Sparta, Rome). Furthermore, in times past, such régimes have tended to degenerate into government by armed mobs (praetorians, janissaries), which can do nothing but squander wealth.

2275. II. *Governments relying chiefly on intelligence and cunning.*

II-a. If the intelligence and cunning are used chiefly to influence sentiments, the result is some type of theocratic government. The type has entirely disappeared in our Western countries and on it therefore we need not linger. The governments of the ancient kings in Greece and in Italy may have approximated the type, in some respects at least; but we know too little of their history to be warranted in so asserting.

II-b. If the intelligence and cunning are used chiefly to play upon interests—which, however, does not necessarily imply disregard of sentiments—the result is governments like the demagogic régimes in Athens, the rule of the Roman aristocracy at various moments under the Republic, the governments of many mediaeval republics, and finally the very important type of government flourishing in our day—government by "speculators."

2276. All governments of the II type, even governments confining the use of intelligence and cunning to playing upon sentiments, have governing classes in which Class I residues predominate as compared with Class II residues. For to play artfully, shrewdly, and with success upon both interests and sentiments requires a governing class possessing combination instincts in high degree and unencumbered with too many scruples. Class-circulation is generally slow in the subtype II-a, but rapid, sometimes very rapid, in subtype II-b. It attains its maximum velocity under the system of our contemporary speculators. Governments of the II-a type are usually inexpensive, but they produce very little. They stupefy their populations, moreover, and kill every stimulus to economic production. Making no great use of force, they cannot make up for deficiencies in home production by wealth acquired through conquests abroad. In fact they fall ready prey to neighbour countries expert in the use of force and so disappear either by conquest or by internal decay. II-b governments are expensive, oftentimes very very expensive, but they produce actively and sometimes enormously, so that there may be such an excess of production over costs as to assure great prosperity. But there is no guarantee that as expenditures increase the surplus will not shrink to much lower proportions, disappear, and perhaps even change to a deficit. That depends on numberless conditions and circumstances. Such régimes may degenerate into government by shrewd but cowardly individuals who are easily overthrown by violence, whether from abroad or from within. That was the case with many democratic governments in Greek cities, and it played no inconsiderable part in the fall of the Roman and Venetian republics.

2277. In the concrete one finds combinations of these various types, with now the one, now the other, predominating. Governments in which the II-b type in moderate proportions is combined with a considerable dosage of the I type may endure for a long time on a foundation of force, and without sacrifice of economic prosperity. This mixed type is represented more or less closely by the earlier Roman Empire. It runs the risk of the degeneration peculiar to type I, and of a progressive dwindling in the proportions of the II-b type. Governments in which the II-b type in considerable proportions is combined with the I type in small proportions may also last for a long time, because they have a certain capacity for self-defence while achieving very considerable economic prosperity. They risk the degenerations peculiar to the II-*b* type and a progressive diminution of the type I element; and that almost inevitably exposes them to danger of foreign conquest. That development played its part in the destruction of Carthage and in the conquest of Greece by the Romans.

2278. Governments that rely chiefly on force in their relations represent combinations of the I and II-*b* types. That was more or less the case with the government of the Roman aristocracy in the heyday of the Republic.